DOGS ARE PEOPLE tOO

The Practical Guide to Understanding and

Training Your Dog

(because you're more alike than you think!)

Mary Jean Alsina, CPDT-KA, PCT-A, M.A

Dogs Are People Too
The Practical Guide to Understanding and Training Your Dog
(because you're more alike than you think!)

Copyright ©2016 Mary Jean Alsina

ISBN 978-1506-901-85-5 PRINT

LCCN 2016936852

April 2016

Published and Distributed by
First Edition Design Publishing, Inc.
P.O. Box 20217, Sarasota, FL 34276-3217
www.firsteditiondesignpublishing.com

TABLE OF CONTENTS

Acknowledgments

As you can imagine, undertaking something like writing a book is not a simple task by any means. The support that I have received from various people must be acknowledged because without them, this book would not be here.

First and foremost, I would be nowhere without the support of my husband, Izzy. When I first began my road into the dog training world and started my business, I had no idea how it would pan out. Izzy stood behind me the whole way. Although he never verbalized it, I knew he was nervous about how it would pay the bills, but here we are. Without his belief in me and unending support, traveling this amazing, successful road and completing this book would not have been possible. I love him now and forever and thank him from the bottom of my heart for standing by me.

To my son, Jason, I thank him for being such an inspiration in the writing of this book. Without even knowing it, he helped me develop many of the ideas and provided many "light bulb" moments for me as the book progressed. He is one of my biggest cheerleaders when it comes to my business and I am an extremely fortunate mother to have him as my son.

To Bob Martin, my longest and closest friend, who has been my cheerleader since day one and someone who taught me about unconditional love. Sarcasm and all, I love him and thank him for always standing by my side.

To John Visconti, who is one of the best friends and mentors anyone could hope for. The amount of information I have learned from him over the years is endless and the friendship we have is irreplaceable.

To Susan Nilson, my wonderful editor, who helped me realize how to take my time and do things the right way. She is a brilliant, kind, and talented woman that helped me more than she knows in the writing of this book. I owe her a lifetime full of rice milk and vegan cupcakes!

To Sierra, my darling bomb-proof rescue dog. I consider myself to have hit the jackpot rescuing a dog like her considering she was found wandering the streets. She is smart, sweet, affectionate, hardworking, and welcomes every dog we pet sit into our home like she's known them forever. I learn from her every day and love her to bits.

To Jackie, Angel, and Pharaoh, my sweet canine angels. I miss them every day and they will always have a huge piece of my heart.

To Tanya, Steve, every force-free trainer out there in the trenches, and the Pet Professional Guild, all of whom are hard at work every single day to show that science-based training for all sentient beings is the only way forward – for so many reasons.

To every dog and owner that I have had the pleasure of working with, you have all contributed to this book more than you know and I thank you for allowing me to be a part of your life now as you were a part of mine. I love you all!

How the Relationship Began

"We see dog behavior and human behavior as a convergence. Dogs became similar to humans because they had to live in a human social environment. This will tell us quite a lot about human social evolution."

— Dr. Ádám Miklósi,
Director of the Family Dog Project and head of ethology,
Eötvös Loránd University, Budapest, Hungary (n.d.)

How many times do you feel like you are dealing with a child (or spouse for that matter) when you are getting frustrated with your dog? Do you find yourself saying, "Stop that, Jason!" instead of "Stop that, Fido!" and vice versa? Do you feel that Fido does things "on purpose" just to irritate you like, say, a co-worker might? Do you feel like you need the canine equivalent of Supernanny to help you out? In fact, Supernanny could be just what you need given that the sheer number of uncanny similarities between human and canine behavior is becoming more apparent as the body of research grows. Scientists and canine behavior professionals are finding increasingly that dogs behave more like their human counterparts than we may care to admit. Now, I won't go getting all anthropomorphic on you, but the facts are there. If you can successfully navigate through many human issues, you can apply the same techniques to your four-legged friend with great success. As a result, you will achieve more fulfilling relationships in both the canine and human areas of your life.

This is not a book on how to train your dog to sit or stay. Nor am I going to delve into a million reasons as to why dog training these days is, tragically, split down the middle when it comes to philosophies. What this book will do instead is clearly lay out how you can approach your understanding of human and dog relationships in a very similar fashion and find increased success in both. If I had a nickel for every time a client asked me if I can

i

clicker* train husbands or kids, I would be a millionaire! The answer is yes, you can. I have used clickers in lectures with humans and witnessed the same smiles and excitement that I get from dogs while training. Humans don't necessarily need to see the clicker, but the scientific principles work beautifully and can be applied in virtually any context. You can use the principles of canine and human behavior in many areas to achieve similar, and, more importantly, desirable results.

It is commonly accepted that dogs became domesticated over a period of thousands of years. Some believe that not only did humans domesticate dogs, but that dogs actually had a hand in domesticating humans too. Dogs were the first domesticated animals with whom humans developed a close attachment.

According to certified applied animal behaviorist and renowned author, Dr. Karen Overall (2016), human and dog cognition "seems similar, and humans and dogs have virtually identical social systems. Dogs' cognition appears similar to humans' (consider co-evolution) and they can learn by watching both other dogs and humans."

At the 2015 Pet Professional Guild Summit in Tampa, Florida where Overall gave the keynote address, she admitted that she was not taken very seriously when she first brought up this concept many years ago. Groves (1999) meanwhile, despite much criticism, states that humans were domesticated as a result of the actions of dogs: "The human-dog relationship amounts to a very long lasting symbiosis. Dogs acted as humans' alarm systems, trackers, and hunting aides, garbage disposal facilities, hot water bottles, and children's guardians and playmates. Humans provided dogs with food and security. The relationship was stable over 100,000 years or so, and intensified in the Holocene into mutual domestication. Humans domesticated dogs and dogs domesticated humans."

In comparison to other primates, humans that lived thousands of years ago have been shown to experience an actual decrease in certain senses because they relied heavily on their dogs to do certain tasks for them, such as sniffing out the scents of prey and alerting to approaching or impending danger. This has been observed through the brain shrinkage evident in the areas of the brain dedicated to these specific senses. Dogs' brains meanwhile, have decreased 20 percent in size due to the loss of tissue in the areas used for learning and cognition. While humans were relying on dogs to take care of audio and olfactory needs, dogs were counting on the humans to do their fair share of thinking for them in return. Since the canine brain has decreased in size due to domestication, Groves would lead us to believe that the human brain must also have shrunk, due to dogs' reciprocal domestication of us.

"Surprisingly, human brains have actually shrunk, but by only a tenth, suggesting that dogs got more out of the deal than we did," says Groves (1999).

*"Clicker training" is a method of training animals (or humans) based on the psychology of behavior in which a desired behavior is observed, immediately followed by a click to mark the behavior, followed by a reward to reinforce the likelihood of the behavior being repeated.

CHAPTER 1

The Hierarchy of Needs

"The fact is that people are good. Give people affection and security, and they will give affection and be secure in their feelings and their behavior." - Maslow (n.d.)

These words of brilliance came from Abraham Maslow, an American psychologist who was born in Brooklyn, New York and lived from 1908-1970. Between being the victim of anti-Semitism and despising his own mother, Maslow had quite a rough childhood. In his own words about his mother, Maslow states, "What I had reacted to was not only her physical appearance, but also her values and world view, her stinginess, her total selfishness, her lack of love for anyone else in the world–even her own husband and children–her narcissism, her Negro prejudice, her exploitation of everyone, her assumption that anyone was wrong who disagreed with her, her lack of friends, her sloppiness and dirtiness..." (Maslow (n.d.) cited in Hoffman (1988)). In spite of all this, through his love of books, libraries, and learning, Maslow rose up and went on to become one of history's most well-known psychologists.

In conjunction with American psychologists Carl Rogers and Rollo May, Maslow laid the groundwork for what is known as humanistic psychology, or positive psychology. Humanistic psychology puts the power of self-improvement into the hands of the individual. In contrast to Sigmund Freud, the Austrian neurologist, and B.F. Skinner, the renowned American psychologist, Maslow felt strongly that people are inherently good and that freewill takes on a large role in a human's existence. He stated that it is as if Freud supplied us the "sick half of psychology and we must now fill it out with the healthy half." (Maslow, 1968). In 1954, in his book *Motivation and Personality*, Maslow unveiled what is widely known as *Maslow's Hierarchy of Needs*. He strongly believed that humans would only resort to violence when their needs were not met. He did not believe that people "wanted" to cheat, steal, lie, commit murder, or the like. On the contrary, if the needs of a human were sufficiently met, Maslow believed that he or she would lean towards love and growth.

Maslow's
Hierarchy of Needs

SELF-
ACTUALIZA-
TION
morality, creativity,
spontaneity, acceptance,
experience purpose, meaning
and inner potential

SELF-ESTEEM
confidence, achievement, respect of others,
the need to be a unique individual

LOVE AND BELONGING
friendship, family, intimacy, sense of connection

SAFETY AND SECURITY
health, employment, property, family and social abilty

PHYSIOLOGICAL NEEDS
breathing, food, water, shelter, clothing, sleep

(Photo: Elenarts/Shutterstock.com)

The various levels of the *Hierarchy of Needs* clearly lay out what Maslow believed to be the path to human self-actualization. For me as a professional dog trainer, this automatically leads to the question, can dogs self-actualize the way humans do? The research is still out on that one, but we know for sure that they can problem solve and grow to their fullest potential as we, or they, may see it. Let's break down each level in the hierarchy and look into how it pertains to humans, as well as dogs, so we can see the tremendous similarities between human and canine needs.

Physiological Needs

Before anything else can be achieved, humans must have certain needs met. They require food, air, water, shelter, warmth, and sleep, among others. If I try to talk to my husband when he is hungry, I know my efforts will be completely futile. I have learned to wait until he has eaten, then approach him with whatever needs to be discussed. Would I like to be able to not have to wait for him to eat? Of course! But I know I will get nowhere without his hunger being relieved. It's worth the wait. Think about how often food and drink is available when you attend a work meeting. Bosses clearly know that in order to function well, humans must have these certain needs met. Try to talk to a non-morning person when they first wake up feeling grumpy and sleep-deprived, then let me know how that goes for you. Give that person a delicious breakfast and a cup full of caffeine and you may achieve different results. These physiological needs are the basis and structure for moving up through the hierarchy.

Dogs, like us, also have very critical basic needs that should be met before we can expect anything further from them. Dogs require proper nutrition, fresh water and oxygen, an adequate amount of sleep, an appropriate place to relieve themselves, regular veterinary care, a safe place to sleep, shelter, and exercise.

Feeding a dog a cheap, low-quality brand of food is assuredly not as healthy as feeding a higher quality food and many dogs will display changes in behavior depending on the food they eat. This is literally step one towards getting your dog on the right path. You cannot fill a gas tank of a car with ketchup and expect it to run correctly. You need what the car was intended to run on, which is of course, gasoline. Dogs are not meant to function on "food" made with preservatives, roadkill, euthanized animals, and other undesirable materials, which is what many dog food ingredients contain today. To function optimally, dogs require a well-balanced, natural, healthy diet and deserve no less. They also deserve fresh water and fresh air. A dog locked up inside all day will (most likely) go nuts! Dogs need to get out and smell the roses, just like we do.

Sleep is also essential for dogs. Tired dogs need to sleep and, if deprived of this, can become quite cranky just like people can.

Dogs need to rejuvenate and refresh from the activities that have tired them. There is a reason that sleep deprivation is used as a form of punishment because that is exactly what it is. If you have young children running around a tired dog that needs sleep, the dog should have a safe haven away from the action, possibly in a crate in another room, to rest and relax. Forcing a dog to put up with the noisy children is not, in any way, fair or humane in such a context.

Dogs also require an appropriate place to eliminate and regular veterinary care. Some owners, like myself, choose to be less invasive when it comes to vet care, but vet trips are still important for check-ups or if immediate medical care is necessary.

As a trainer, I see on a daily basis that exercise is one of the most overlooked and underrated physiological need for dogs (and humans). The benefits of exercise to both species are undeniable. Some of the benefits of exercise for dogs are that it:

> Reduces or eliminates chewing, digging, barking, scratching.

> Keeps a healthy weight – so many dogs are couch potatoes today.

> Reduces digestive problems.

> Aids fearful dogs in building self-confidence and trust.

> Helps keep the body limber and agile.

> Countless others.

I know if I don't take my 3-year-old pit bull Sierra out to run a couple times a day (10-15 minutes each time), she will drive me insane! Sierra is a fun-loving, energetic, and playful pup who enjoys a long romp in the park followed by a nice snooze on the couch. I rescued her in the fall of 2015 and she has been a wonderful addition to our family, but if her exercise needs are not

4

met, I can be sure she will let me know in a way that I am not happy with.

"If your dog is fat, you're not getting enough exercise." – Unknown

(Photo: Phatthanit/Shutterstock.com)

Safety

Something I have always been terrified of is upside down rollercoasters. Does that mean I have never been on one? No. Did I go on them willingly? Heck no. These rollercoaster riding experiences, by the way, were brought about by oodles of persuasion by my husband. Did I enjoy it? I am still not sure. Was I glad it was over? Absolutely! While I sat in the seat with the bars placed over me so I would not be ejected (my mind was creating all sorts of frightening scenarios), I was feeling sheer terror. My stomach was in knots and there was no way I could even think about eating, talking, or anything for that matter. I just wanted it over. I was "over threshold" as we say when dogs are experiencing fear. All I wanted was to flee the scene and get to safety. My husband comforted me and attempted to make me laugh, which assisted me in calming a bit.

For humans to feel safe, we need to feel security at home and at work, have financial security, health, stability, security of resources, family and property. Both dogs and humans need to feel safe from perceived threats. Dogs, as well as humans, function in fight or flight mode. Without safety, nothing can be achieved. No learning, no self-confidence, no fun, nada. An animal must feel safe in order to learn.

There is no way that I could learn anything sitting waiting for that rollercoaster to start. All I could think of was how scared I was, how I wanted to feel safe, and how desperately I wanted the ride to be over. When the brain senses a threat of any kind, it immediately changes the way it normally channels information. The logical part of the brain basically starts to short-circuit and overload the limbic system, which regulates the emotions.

Dr. Bruce Perry, senior fellow of The Child Trauma Academy, located in Houston, Texas, says, "The fear or alarm response, however, kills curiosity and inhibits exploration and learning. If people are anxious, uncomfortable, or fearful, they do not learn...When we feel threat of any kind—hunger, thirst, pain, shame, confusion, or information that is too much, too new, or too fast—our body and mind respond in ways designed to keep us safe. Our mind focuses only on the information that is, at that moment, important for responding to the threat." (Perry, 2006). This works the same for animals and is exactly why dogs (and humans) are unable to learn and function optimally when fearful.

Dog safety comes in various forms:

➢ Structure (the dog knows he will be getting what he needs in terms of food, water, schedule, etc.).

➢ An environment that enables the dog to feel safe and not feel forced to protect himself from perceived or potential harm.

➢ Humans that understand the language the dog speaks (body language) so the lines of communication stay open and the dog can look to the owner for guidance when fear is taking hold.

➤ The ability to learn coping skills and be taught these in a patient manner.

"Quick but sometimes wrong is better than slow and sometimes dead." These are brilliant words indeed, as stated by Joseph Ledoux (n.d), professor of psychology and neuroscience at New York University and expert in the workings of the brain as a result of fear and anxiety. If a dog does not feel safe, it is not possible for learning to happen. If you are walking your dog and he sees another dog that scares him, do not expect him to be able to listen to you if he is reacting. He has already entered fight or flight mode and no learning will occur until he is brought under threshold at what he perceives to be a safe distance away from the other dog. THAT is where the learning can begin and where your dog will begin to listen to you. Ledoux further explains that "severe threats to well-being activate hard wired circuits in the brain and produce responses that help us survive." (Ledoux (n.d.) cited in Szalavitz (2013)).

According to Szalavitz (2013), this process is the "most important thing for the organism at the moment, and brain resources are monopolized to achieve the goal of coping with the threat." It is so common to see an owner with a dog that is absolutely terrified being dragged towards whatever is scaring him, which, in the terminology of behavior, is known as "flooding." Many owners think that the dog just has to "get used to it." It would be a beautiful thing if it worked this way but, unfortunately, it does not. Every once in a while, a dog may habituate to something he is bothered by, but in most cases flooding the dog will only make the fear get worse. An example of habituation is a home located next to railroad tracks. When visiting someone at their house you may think, "How can they possibly live with all this noise?" But in fact, what has occurred is habituation, which simply means the residents have become accustomed to the situation. Only when a dog feels safe and secure in his world can the next step up the hierarchy begin, which is love and belonging.

(Photo: Fongleon356/Shutterstock.com)

This dog is being flooded as he is being pulled towards something from which he is attempting to distance himself.

Love and Belonging

We all need and want to be loved and feel as if we belong in some way. Maslow states that love and belonging can be achieved after physiological and safety needs have been met. Love and belonging can include overcoming loneliness, alienation, and isolation, feeling part of a family, friendships, and being included in a group. Well, it turns out that dogs desire these as well and love us just as much as we love them! Is that pit bull who almost wiggles her butt off when you come in the house really showing you love? When your Labrador takes a running leap into your arms after not seeing you for five seconds, is he showing "dominance" (which of course, has been disproven as dogs are not wolves so cannot be expected to function the same way) or love? Numerous studies have been conducted to date and shown what we have wished for all along, namely, for our dogs to love us.

Animal cognition scientists at Emory University in Atlanta, Georgia trained dogs to lie completely still in MRI machines and

DOGS ARE PEOPLE TOO

employed functional magnetic resonance imaging (fMRI) to measure their brain activity in response to the smells of familiar and unfamiliar dogs and humans. The studies, led by neuroscientist and author of *How Dogs Love Us*, Gregory Berns, showed that the smell of the dog's owner triggered arousal in the caudate nucleus, or the "reward center" of the brain. Of all the aromas that were presented to the dogs, they preferred the smell of "their" human to any other. These tests concurred with other researchers' findings as well. Researchers at Eötvös Loránd University in Budapest, Hungary conducted studies in which sounds, not smells, were presented to still dogs in an MRI machine. The study showed how similarly humans and dogs process vocal sounds that are emotionally charged. Happy sounds were shown to lighten up the auditory cortex in dogs and humans. This is why I always stress to clients how important tone of voice is when interacting with a dog (and people, for that matter). Yelling at a dog or person creates fear. Plain and simple.

"In short: Dogs don't just *seem* to pick up on our subtle mood changes — they are actually physically wired to pick up on them," says Fisher (2014). I tell clients to call their dog an asshole if they are frustrated but say it in an upbeat tone that will not create fear. It is a win-win. The owner feels better and their dog loves them for whispering sweet nothings to them.

Behavior studies support these MRI studies and also show that dogs act with their owners as babies do with their parents. Dogs, like young children - in contrast to many other species - run desperately to their owners when they are scared, while cats and horses are known to run away when fearful. Dogs are also the only non-primates to look into humans' eyes and actually seek out eye contact, yet they do not do this with their biological canine parents. Attila Andics, a Hungarian neuroscientist and the lead researcher for these studies, states that, "Bonding with owners is much more important for dogs than other pets." (Andics, Gácsi, Faragó, Kis, & Miklósi, 2014).

Equally as important as love is a feeling of belonging. Many dogs thoroughly enjoy being included in family activities as much as possible. I know when my family and I are getting ready to go out, Sierra tears frantically to the front door grinning ear to ear with excitement and wonder of where our next adventure will take her. She absolutely loves being with us and I try to take her to work with me most days. She rides in the car and while I train my clients' dogs, she naps in my air-conditioned, locked car. In between appointments we find a park for her to run. She simply loves being with me as much as possible and many dogs are the same way. Dogs are social animals and love to be a part of the family. Play with them, train, cuddle, take them hiking, jogging, to the park, to the beach, and anywhere they are allowed. More and more places are becoming pet-friendly and this is even further reason to get your dog well-trained so he can become a frequent companion on your daily travels!

(Photo: Mary Jean Alsina)

Sierra's second day in our home. From day one,
we made her feel like a part of the family.

(Photo: Mary Jean Alsina)

My son, Jason, and his little sister soon after she joined our family.

Esteem

In humans, Maslow characterizes esteem as the need to have self-respect and the desire to be highly regarded by others. Being confident and recognized for one's accomplishments can also be included in this level of the hierarchy. As humans, it is always nice to be acknowledged for our accomplishments and this helps raise our self-esteem. Of course, we should not <u>require</u> the admiration of others in order to have high self-esteem. There is a difference between enjoying respect and admiration from others and not being able to survive or function without their approval.

This level for dogs involves confidence, independence, self-esteem, lack of fearful behaviors, and the ability to take risks. Have you ever seen the joy of a dog who has done something for the first time and made his owner ecstatically happy? How about a dog who is slowly learning to trust the world around him and does something new and risky on his time clock and not because he was forced into it? There is nothing more fulfilling than witnessing that.

Some examples of this may include:

> A dog using his brain to figure out a puzzle toy.

> A previously fearful dog doing something new with self-assurance.

> Graduating a reactive dog class.

> Winning a dog show.

(Photo: Sergey Lavrentev/Shutterstock.com)

Here is a dog after winning a show.
Looks like a happy dog to me.

Not only can we, as owners, help raise our dogs' self-esteem, according to studies, but they do quite the same in return. Researchers at Oxford Ohio College in Miami, Florida found that pets render as much support as parents and siblings and were only outscored by best friends. The study also determined that pet owners spoil their pets as much as they do because the pets make them so ridiculously happy (McConnell, Brown, Shoda, Stayton, & Martin, 2011). For me, I know if I come home with one more toy or bone for Sierra, my husband may ask for a divorce! Yes, I spoil my dog, so sue me.

How do we kill our dogs' self-esteem? By quitting on them and assuming they are "stupid" because they do not get something right the first time due to lack of proper teaching or some other reason. I hear owners occasionally refer to their dog as stupid. No dog is stupid. Do some dogs learn quicker than others? Of course, but that does not make one dog stupid and another brilliant. The "stupid" dog just needs to be taught in a way that he can understand, just like a human being. Any being that can detect cancer, sniff out bodies miles away, wake up someone suffering from post-traumatic stress disorder who is having a nightmare, or alert of an impending heart attack or stroke does not classify as stupid in my book.

Self-Actualization

For humans, self-actualization is reaching our highest potential. Maslow includes morality, self-fulfillment, and seeking personal growth in this process and describes it further as, "What a man *can* be, he *must* be. This need we may call self-actualization... It refers to the desire for self-fulfillment, namely, to the tendency for him to become actualized in what he is potentially. This tendency might be phrased as the desire to become more and more what one is, to become everything that one is capable of becoming." (Maslow, 1954).

The characteristics of a self-actualized person are that he or she:

➢ Embraces the unknown and the ambiguous.
➢ Accepts him- or herself with all flaws.
➢ Prioritizes, enjoys the journey, not just the destination.
➢ Does not seek to shock or disturb.
➢ Is motivated by growth, not by the satisfaction of needs.
➢ Has purpose.

- Is not troubled by small things.
- Is grateful.
- Shares deep relationships with a few, but also feels identification and affection towards the entire human race.
- Is humble.
- Resists enculturation.
- Is not perfect.

We know, at least at this point in science, that some of these are not possible for dogs, but most of them can be applied, to an extent at least, to how dogs function throughout life. Most dogs that are not neophobic or do not have fears towards certain stimuli can deal with new situations successfully. Most dogs, as we know, live in the moment and definitely enjoy the journey. Sierra continues to teach me this lesson day after day and I am slowly learning (she probably thinks *I'm* the stupid one for not learning it quickly enough). Watch a dog with an interactive feeding toy and tell me he does not have purpose. Many dogs definitely become bonded with a select few but can show affection to many. Dogs certainly are not perfect and some seem to even find joy and excitement when not being perfect, especially when we are laughing at them. Some dogs almost seem to rise to the occasion of attempting to garner more laughter.

Many people think that dogs feel gratitude, especially dogs that have been rescued from shelters or off the street. More research is still necessary on this topic, but it is understandable that the looks, kisses, and affection these dogs give us could lead us to believe that they are forever grateful. Other applications of self-actualization for dogs include creativity, problem-solving, and using the ability of humans to help them reach their highest potential. It is our duty as owners to provide this for our dogs, just as we would our children. They deserve it.

There are also studies that show dogs may display some type of morality while being observed in play. Cognitive ethologist Marc Bekoff is a professor emeritus at the University of Colorado at Boulder where he taught for 32 years. Bekoff spent four years intensively studying videos of dogs, wolves, and coyotes playing. He watched every single body movement and analyzed each motion as to what it could possibly denote. He was not solely focused on the play and the behavior during the play, but on the emotions surrounding the play and what was occurring in the animals' brains.

Even back in the 1800s, Charles Darwin, an English naturalist and geologist, alluded to the fact that dogs were capable of displaying morality and even language, but many disagreed with him. Bekoff, while scrutinizing the play of these animals, saw behaviors that led him to believe that dogs possibly can display morality and much higher level thinking than was previously thought. He identified the "play bow," which involves the dog's rump up in the air and front legs down on the ground. Dogs use this signal as an invitation to play. What Bekoff also found interesting was the self-handicapping often implemented by dogs. For example, a Rottweiler playing with a Yorkshire terrier may elect to "take it easy" on the smaller dog because of the size difference. The larger dog may roll on his back and allow the petite dog to jump on him rather than crush him with his body.

The dog on the right is in a play bow, which is a meta signal. This is an invitation to play in dog language. Dogs use meta signals in play which lets other dogs know they mean no harm. Dogs may implement a play bow before biting on another's dog's neck in play, for example. Humans use meta signals all the time. A person can insult another but use a tone and manner that lets the other know they are joking and mean no harm.

(Photo: Be Good/Shutterstock.com)

(Photo: DragoNika/Shutterstock.com)

*This picture shows self-handicapping as the larger
dogs are taking care to not hurt the little dog.*

"In the wild, coyotes ostracize pack members that don't play by the rules. Something similar happens in dog parks: If three dogs are playing and one bites or tackles too hard, the other two are likely to give him the cold shoulder and stop playing with him," states Bekoff. Such behavior, Bekoff says, suggests that dogs are capable of morality, a mindset once thought to be uniquely human. (Bekoff, 2015).

"Even morality hints at something deeper, however," says Grimm (2014). "To enforce moral conduct, dogs must be able to experience a spectrum of emotions, from joy to indignation, guilt to jealousy. They must also be able to read these emotions in others, distinguishing accident from intent, honesty from deceit. And indeed, recent studies by other scientists have shown evidence of these abilities (confirming what many dog owners already feel about their pets)." (Grimm, 2014).

Scientists have also found that dogs, like numerous other species, have been shown to display empathy as they are quick to nuzzle and lick distressed humans. Bekoff has found that dogs exhibit the capacity to know what another animal is thinking. For example, if one dog is attempting to engage another dog in play and does not have the other dog's attention, he will take measures to get this attention in order to start play. The playful dog knows the other one is not paying attention to him and will nip or bark at him to get him to play. This is reminiscent of child play or the persistence of a man hitting on a woman in a bar, is it not? Dogs have been also shown to fare better on certain tests than chimpanzees. In tests conducted, if a scientist pointed at one of two cups, a dog would run to the cup to which the scientist pointed, showing comprehension for what the scientist was thinking and what task was expected. Chimpanzees, on the other hand, seemed to have no idea as to what the scientists were doing when pointing to the cups. Brian Hare, a biological anthropologist at Duke University in Durham, North Carolina and one of the world's most well-known experts on canine cognition, was one of the first scientists to show that dogs could understand human pointing, while chimps could not.

Hare states, "What we know for certain is that the cognitive world of every dog is far more complex and interesting than we thought possible...It is not always obvious where dogs will show an ability to make inferences or show more flexibility than other species. But in the end, your intuition is correct-your dog is a genius." (Hare, 2013). Looking into a dog's complex thinking even further, Bekoff says that what is "really nice about studying play and fun in dogs is that you can see all of the above at your local dog park. When we study play and fun we're really studying ourselves as well. And, it's fun to do. It's a win-win for all involved." (Bekoff, 2015).

Let's now start to delve into how these similarities really show up in our day-to-day lives and how we can gain a better understanding of our dogs' behavior.

Chapter 2

How Are We Like Our Canine Buddies?

(Photo: Deborah Kolb/Shutterstock.com)

(Photo: Halfpoint/Shutterstock.com)

(Photo: Everett Collection/Shutterstock.com)

Do you look like your dog? Well, you may or may not but you probably act like him more than you realize or care to admit. Am I calling you a dog? Not really, but what might surprise you is the vast similarities between humans and canines that are being proven every day through science. Now I am not saying by any means that dogs have human levels of intelligence. Well-known canine researcher, Stanley Coren Ph.D. at the University of British Columbia in Vancouver, Canada has concluded that dogs have the ability to reach a higher level of thinking to problem solve. Coren says that many tests show dogs to have an intelligence level on par with a 2-2 ½ year old child. Through Coren's tests, it was determined that average dogs can learn up to 165 words and signals, while some dogs, such as border collies, can learn up to 250 words. Dogs can also count to four or five and detect mathematical errors in simple problems such as 1+1= 3.

"Four studies Coren examined looked [at] how dogs solve spatial problems by modeling human or other dogs' behavior using a barrier type problem. Through observation, Coren said, dogs can learn the location of valued items (treats), better routes in the environment (the fastest way to a favorite chair), how to operate mechanisms (such as latches and simple machines) and the meaning of words and symbolic concepts (sometimes by simply listening to people speak and watching their actions)." (American Psychological Association, 2009).

According to Coren (2009), dogs during play are capable of deliberately trying to deceive other dogs and people in order to get rewards. "And they are nearly as successful in deceiving humans as humans are in deceiving dogs," says Coren. Yeah, they're stupid. Right.

Dogs have many other talents, of which many people may not be aware. Studies have shown that dogs can read human facial expressions, exhibit jealousy, show empathy, and watch television. I have worked with a number of clients whose dogs literally lose their minds when they see dogs or other animals on television. These characteristics were amassed as part of the domestication process that began thousands and thousands of years ago.

"Don't worry that children never listen to you; worry that they are always watching you."

- Robert Fulghum (n.d.)

This is a pertinent quote for any adult because children ARE watching. All. The. Time. Sorry to scare you, but so are your dogs. That "stupid" dog is watching every single move you make. Why do you think he wants to follow you in the bathroom every time nature calls? He wants to know why you are not peeing on a tree outside like he does. Okay, maybe not, but dogs are utilizing what is labeled "social eavesdropping" and are not the only species to employ this tool. Dogs, as well as humans, appear to use social eavesdropping, or people watching, as a way of determining who is kind and whom they may want to avoid. Could this be why your dog barks and lunges at random people on the street? He may be sensing something that we possibly cannot.

In a recent study by Chijiwa, Kuroshima, Hori, Anderson, and Fajita (2015), scientists worked with 54 dogs who were made to watch their owners attempt to remove a roll of tape from a container with some difficulty. The dogs were divided into three groups: a helper group, a non-helper group, and a control group. The helper group consisted of the owner, who received help from another person who held the tape container for them. The non-helper group involved the owner struggling and another person who turned their back on the owner when asked for help. The third, or control group had the extra person turn their back before they were asked for assistance. In addition, for each experiment, there was a neutral person present in the room during the study.

After the first experiment, the neutral party and the helper or non-helper offered treats to the dog. In the non-helper group, dogs most often chose the neutral party's treat, ignoring the non-helper. Yet in the helper group, the dogs showed no favoritism to the helper or the neutral person. The question being studied was, 'Do dogs snub people who are mean to their owners?' The jury is still out on this one, but the studies thus far lean toward dogs exhibiting the human quality of discerning nice from unkind.

Jealous Much?

Elsewhere, scientists have confirmed that dogs do, in fact, exhibit jealous tendencies just like we do. A study conducted at the University of California in San Diego concluded that dogs are fully capable of eliciting jealous-type behaviors. Dogs and their owners were placed in individual rooms with three different objects – an animatronic dog, a pumpkin, and a pop-up children's musical book. When owners showed attention to the fake dog, the real canines were more thoroughly agitated and were twice more likely to attempt to secure the attention of the owner than when the owner gave attention to the pumpkin or children's book. The dogs snapped at and nipped the fake dog and tried to push in between the owner and the fake dog. I bet that you know at least one dog that does this body-blocking move!

Countless times, I hear from owners that their dog tries to push in between two people if they are hugging, or one dog attempts to push the other dog out of the way if he is getting affection from the owner. I know when I am pet sitting, Sierra loves to have the sleepovers and play with the other dogs, but if I am petting or cuddling one of those dogs, she is right there in the middle trying to break it up like a jealous girlfriend. It is adorable! Not all dogs are like this though and, as we will see later on, dogs

MARY JEAN ALSINA

have a variety of temperaments and levels of tolerance, just like people do.

"Many people have assumed that jealousy is a social construction of human beings, or that it's an emotion specifically tied to sexual and romantic relationships," says the University of California at San Diego's Christine Harris, one of the researchers in the aforementioned study. "Our results challenge these ideas, showing that animals besides ourselves display strong distress whenever a rival usurps a loved one's affection." (Harris and Prouvost, 2014).

The Happy Center of the Brain

The MRIs that were taken of the dogs trained by neuroscientist Gregory Berns and his team showed remarkable similarities in the human brain compared to the canine brain, specifically in the "reward center," or caudate nucleus. Humans' caudate nuclei are triggered by enjoyable things such as food or music. In canines, the caudate nucleus was activated by many of the same things that make the human brain happy. Berns (2013) states that this does not necessarily mean that dogs feel emotions exactly like humans, but it certainly displays the numerous similarities. After the conclusion of this MRI study at Emory University, Berns genuinely felt that dogs should have enhanced legal rights due to the overwhelming research validating how similar to humans they actually are.

According to Millstein (2014), in one "exhaustive" Hungarian study (conducted by Soproni, et.al. (2001)), scientists observed "so many similarities between dogs and humans that they suggested dogs, not chimpanzees, should be considered humans' closest analogue. Much of this has to do with social behavior: Human groups act much more similarly to groups of dogs than groups of chimpanzees."

Humans have been shown to exhibit three main kinds of social behavior. These are:

> Sociality – when people in a group are loyal and less aggressive toward each other.

22

➢ Synchronization – when people follow shared rules and take on each other's emotions to strengthen the group.

➢ Constructive activity – when members cooperate, communicate, and collaborate to accomplish group goals.

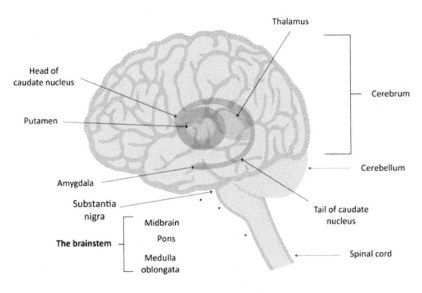

(Photo: Joshya/Shutterstock.com)

Diagram of the human brain, showing the location of the caudate nucleus

The graphic shows the caudate nucleus, or the reward center of the brain. The caudate nucleus is part of the basal ganglia which is a cluster of brain cells at the base of the brain responsible for certain motor movements, such as tying a shoe or playing a musical instrument.

After humans evolved from chimpanzees millions of years ago, the above characteristics were developed. It appears that dogs have learned from humans as they display the exact same group dynamics. Another way that human and canine brains are similar is in the way sounds are perceived. In Andics' MRI studies, dogs were given various sounds to listen to such as human voices, car sounds, and dog vocalizations. Similar parts of the canine and the human brain were triggered when the sounds were heard. "When human voices were played, the temporal pole lit up. When emotionally-charged human sounds, like crying and laughter, were played, an area near the primary auditory cortex lit up. Even emotional dog noises, like barking or whimpering, activated the same neural centers in canines and people. We know very well that dogs are very good at tuning into the feelings of their owners, and we know a good dog owner can detect emotional changes in his dog - but we now begin to understand why this can be." (Andics et al., 2014).

Again, the similarities are extraordinary in so many ways.

CHAPTER 3

Putting the Physiological Similarities to Use in Training

Basic Needs of Humans and Dogs

There are countless ways in which dogs and humans are similar physiologically, but for the purposes of this book we will be focusing on some of the most significant ones. Improving your understanding of your dog's behavior can really aid in achieving more of what you want and less of what you do not.

Let's begin with when you first acquire a dog. Dogs do not ask to be bred, purchased, or adopted, just like children do not ask to be born. As a dog parent, we must accept the responsibility of caring for this animal until the end of his life, as opposed to when we grow tired of him, are struggling to find the time to take care of him, or one of the countless other reasons people use to give up their pets. When people have children, they know they are in it for the long haul. This does not mean they wake up one day and suddenly decide that they are tired of the lack of quiet time, or that they do not want to change diapers any longer. Parents (usually) accept the responsibility of bearing a child and know that they must carry it through, no matter how challenging it becomes.

When people decide to bring children into the world they usually realize it will be a big expense, which is why many delay having children for some time. Children need clothing, food, medical care, etc. As they grow, they require entertainment, activities, adequate sleep, social opportunities, schooling, etc. Most people are aware of this and responsible parents will make sure that these are all covered. Compare all this to the family canine. How many dogs do we see whose basic needs are not being met? This can cause all kinds of behavioral issues.

Children and adults need exercise for both physical and mental health. It helps keep weight down, improves mood, and can be a factor in lowering blood pressure, among countless other benefits. Exercise is such an overlooked essential for many humans, but very much so with dogs. Dogs require exercise, some breeds more than others, and they can become frustrated and troublesome without it. If I do not run Sierra on a daily basis, she gets extremely mouthy and jumpy. Even on very busy days I know if I take her for a walk in the morning and then spend 20 minutes to run her and play fetch, it will make my day manageable because one of her crucial needs has been met. I also ensure that I do this later in the day because if she does not burn her energy, it is almost guaranteed that she will get into something she should not.

Exercise comes in many different forms and creativity is a great thing! I have a huge yard but it is not fenced so I have no choice but to be innovative. Some people might feel that a so-called invisible fence may be appropriate here. I firmly believe, however, that such an approach is not only inhumane but risks causing severe behavioral issues.

An invisible fence works by signaling a dog, who is wearing a "special" collar, with a warning beep when he comes too close to an underground wire. If the dog passes the wire, an electric shock is delivered via the collar to prevent him from approaching the perimeter of the fence in the future. Using an invisible fence can cause numerous problems with dogs' behavior and safety. Simply because a dog is supposedly contained by an invisible fence, it does not mean that other animals cannot enter the property. Also, a dog's prey drive will often override the fear of getting an electric shock and cause him to bolt through the "fence" after an unsuspecting squirrel or rabbit. Unfortunately, in many cases, the dog will then be too afraid to return home because of the fear of the shock that awaits him. What can also happen - and I have seen this many times - is that a dog develops a very negative association to what is on the opposite side of the fence. The frustration of not being able to get to a dog or person walking by, combined with the knowledge that approaching the person or dog means hearing a warning beep and/or getting shocked, can start to cause negative emotions in the dog. In many cases this can increase fear and cause aggression.

That kind of aversive approach is off the table for me. Instead, if I have some extra time, I drive 5 minutes to an enclosed field and run there with Sierra. If I am short on time, I have a 50 foot leash that I tie to a tree in my yard and connect to Sierra's harness so we can play fetch in the yard. It is cheap and does the job. If I travel, I always scout out the area on my GPS and find the closest parks. I always bring my 50 foot leash with me. Although Sierra could be off leash, that is not fair to other people and dogs in the area. Dogs should always be on leash in public areas as an unleashed dog can cause problems for other dogs in proximity to them. Some dogs feel uncomfortable with other dogs running up to them and may have fear issues with other dogs. It is common courtesy to keep your dog leashed when there are other people and dogs around so no fights or other problems arise.

You can play fetch, kick a soccer ball, play tug, have two people standing several yards apart and practice calling the dog to come back and forth between them, use a flirt pole, teach the dog to run on the treadmill in a safe and fun way, teach the dog Treibball, ride your bike with the dog trotting next to you, or get some inexpensive agility equipment and have your kids help you teach the dog to go through a tunnel or weave through some poles. There are so many different options and you can make it a family affair. I know the more I involve my son with the play, the less I feel I have to rush through it to get it done to spend time with him alone. It is something we can all enjoy together. Also, feel free to multi-task (which I do quite frequently). If I am running around doing a million things at once, I will have a tug toy in one hand and be playing tug with Sierra as I walk around my house and do my tasks. That is a win-win - I get my chores done and she is getting attention and working off her excess energy at the same time.

Many dogs with a behavior issue, be it simple hyperactivity or something more involved such as aggression, can improve with increased exercise. Studies also show that "dogs lacking exercise usually have poor muscle tone, and are more prone to injury, brain ailments, and bone disorders. They are also more susceptible to developing emotional problems and behavior quirks." (Veterinary Medicine and Biomedical Sciences Texas A&M University, 2012). So get out there and reap the benefits for both you AND your dog by becoming more active.

Another important area is that of veterinary care and husbandry, which can be defined as simply caring for animals. Husbandry includes nail trimming, coat brushing, teeth brushing, and the like. Periodontal disease is the most common clinical condition in dogs and by the age of three, most dogs sadly have signs of periodontal disease (American Veterinary Dental College, 1988). Nails need to be kept short so it does not hurt to walk and the coat should be brushed of dead skin and fur. Babies and children need to be bathed, have their hair brushed, teeth brushed, nails kept clean, etc. Dogs are exactly the same and will stay healthier and happier if these tasks are completed.

The Use of Food in Training

Look in *Entrepreneur* magazine or a variety of business websites and without fail, you will see one way to acquire and retain clients suggested over and over again: Feed them. Make a reservation for lunch or dinner at a nice restaurant and start dazzling those prospective clients. People use food **ALL THE TIME** to motivate each other and themselves. Why do some people work out every day, besides the obvious physical and mental health benefits? For me (and others I know), it is so we can eat more food and even more so, a variety of food that is perhaps not so healthy.

For years sitting in faculty meetings as a teacher, I observed that the principals who provided free snacks translated into happier teachers during the meetings. I worked for one principal who would occasionally stand at the front door with coffee and hot chocolate for the staff on cold days. Why? Because it was motivating and helped put the teachers in a good frame of mind. It encouraged them to work harder because they recognized that they were valued and respected. According to *Forbes* magazine, giving employees free food creates a happier workplace and I would tend to agree. In 2014, a survey of 1,200 employees working in companies of 20 employees or more was conducted by Seamless, an online delivery and takeout service in the United States and United Kingdom.

The survey showed:

> ➤ 60 percent said that having company-provided food around the office "would make them feel more valued and appreciated."

> ➤ More than half said that a free lunch "would strongly influence their decision to accept a job offer."

> ➤ 60 percent said such free lunches would encourage them to chow down with their colleagues.

> ➤ One-third said that free food at meetings would prompt them to attend optional meetings.

For some unknown reason in the dog training world, using food as a reinforcer is looked down upon by some trainers, who do not quite comprehend the science behind animal behavior. Trainers that use food are sometimes called "cookie-tossers," "bribers," and other colorful names. A truly effective trainer understands that if a dog is being bribed to do a behavior, the training is being done incorrectly. In scientific terms, positive reinforcement means adding a reward following a behavior. Implementing this correctly when training a dog helps to increase the frequency of the behavior. Anyone who grasps the science behind training a dog, or any animal for that matter, will understand and embrace the fact that trainers will use the reinforcement that is most valued to a dog. If a dog does not care about doing something, why the heck would he work for it? It is the same for humans. Dogs do not and will not follow orders from humans just because we think they should. That is simply our ego getting in the way. We must lead, motivate, and reinforce the behaviors that we wish for.

(Photo: Halfpoint/Shutterstock.com)

Using food as a reinforcer is extremely effective in training a dog.

I'm Not Feeling Well! Leave Me Alone!

When you are sick, are you your usual chipper self? I know I sure as hell am not! Why would we expect our dogs to be any different? A simple cold can leave a person cranky, irritable, tired, and all around crotchety. They may as well wear a sign that says "Leave Me Alone." Of course, they don't have to do that because they can simply tell people they do not feel well and to kindly let them be. Since dogs have not mastered the English language, they are unable to verbalize when they do not feel well or something hurts. Be in tune with your dog and watch for signs such as not eating, sluggish behavior, or disinterest in things that normally get him excited. Many dogs' owners and families, though, do not pick up on the signs and the dog may then be forced to take it to the next level, which could include growling, snapping, lunging, or, unfortunately, biting.

Growling is a dog's way of communicating that he is uncomfortable so it is very important to listen when he talks to you. Back off immediately. Get a vet check just as you would if you or your child were sick. This way a medical reason can be ruled out for the defensive behavior. If the problem is not medical, then it most likely stems from a behavioral issue and the problem should be dealt with through behavior modification and the assistance of a qualified professional.

(Photo: Eliana Arce/Shutterstock.com)

Sick dog. The facial expression, such as ears down and slightly back, slightly furrowed brow, and "sad" eyes depict that this is a dog that is not feeling well.

If a child would not be scolded or ridiculed for throwing up on the floor when ill, a dog should be treated in a similar manner. A dog should not be made to wear a sign that says, "I threw up on Mom's favorite rug." Do you think Rover WANTED to decorate the rug with his dinner? No, just like a person does not enjoy a tango with the toilet. Remember, if you would not treat yourself or your child this way, the rules should apply to the dog as well. Intelligence-wise, a dog is the equivalent to a 2-2½-year-old child and it is important to bear this in mind at all times.

Also included in the field of physical well-being is medication. Many children and adults these days are on some form of medication for physical or behavioral issues. Nearly 70 percent of Americans are on at least one prescription drug, and more than half take two, according to Mayo Clinic and Olmsted Medical Center researchers. Antibiotics, antidepressants, and painkilling opioids are most commonly prescribed, the study found. Twenty percent of patients are on five or more prescription medications, according to the findings, published online in the journal *Mayo Clinic Proceedings* (Mayo Clinic, 2013).

Regardless of anyone's thoughts on medication, it is a prominent part of our culture. I tend to believe that many conditions can be overcome with some simple diet and lifestyle changes. There are other conditions though, such as depression, that many doctors seem to think cannot be worked through successfully without pharmaceutical help. I always prefer to use nature first but if further help is needed, working with a doctor to find the right prescription to help someone get back on their feet is the logical next step for most. Medication can be a Band-Aid though, and is best combined with behavioral therapy to get to the roots of an issue that a child or adult may be experiencing. The therapy teaches coping mechanisms along with building self-esteem as the journey progresses.

Dogs experience many of the conditions that humans do. For example, canine depression symptoms are very similar to those in people, according to John Ciribassi DVM, former president of the American Veterinary Society of Animal Behavior. "Dogs will become withdrawn. They become inactive. Their eating and sleeping habits often change. They don't participate in the things they once enjoyed," Ciribassi says (Ciribassi (n.d.) cited in Eckstein (2009)). But vets warn those symptoms can also mean a dog has a medical problem, so the first course of action should always be a full check-up by a veterinarian.

"A pet that mopes around and no longer wants to go for walks could simply have pain from arthritis," says Bonnie Beaver, DVM, executive director of the American College of Veterinary Behaviorists (Beaver (n.d.) cited in Eckstein (2009)).

There is a stigma out there about putting people and dogs on medication when it could truly help save them. If nothing else works, medications can help dogs work through their depression. Karen Sueda, DVM, a diplomat of the American College of

Veterinary Behaviorists, says medications for depressed dogs are the same as those used by depressed humans - Paxil, Prozac, and Zoloft. Sueda also uses Clomicalm, an FDA approved drug for the treatment of separation anxiety in dogs. "It's important that people deal with the problem before it gets too bad," Sueda says. "By the time cases get to me, they're bad. But most cases can be successfully treated early on with behavior modification and environmental enrichment, so it doesn't have to get to the point where we need to use drugs." (Sueda (n.d.) cited in Eckstein (2009)). Beaver says it can take up to two months for some drugs to become effective. "But unlike people, who often remain on antidepressants for years, most dogs can get better in six to 12 months and then be taken off the drugs," Beaver says (Beaver (n.d.) cited in Eckstein (2009)).

Dr. Sueda suggests that dogs are a bit more resilient than humans in this respect. She states that medication can help dogs progress much faster than humans, and that they are unlikely to come to rely on it for as long as many people do. Depending on the severity of the problem, though, some dogs do remain on the medication for life. As Dr. Sueda clarifies, early treatment with behavior modification is crucial before a situation grows in severity. The behavior modification should be used to teach the dog coping skills and confidence similar to human behavioral therapy (Sueda (n.d.) cited in Eckstein (2009)).

I Want It, I Want It, I Want it!!

There are many ways that humans, especially those of the younger persuasion, are quite similar to dogs when it comes to wanting things they cannot have. I know if I tell my son he cannot have something, of course he wants it more and will do whatever he can to get it. As a teacher in the classroom for years, I learned to use reverse psychology to win this war. Humans simply want what they cannot have. Growing up as a young girl, I always chased the boys I knew I had no chance of getting. It is the way many humans are wired. This is the main reason I dislike the word "diet" because not being able to have certain foods makes people want them more. I prefer the term "healthy eating." What is at play in these scenarios is known as psychological reactance, which is defined as a force aroused by threats to a person's freedom. Tell me I cannot have it and I want it more.

The least beneficial thing you can do as an owner is leave all your dog's toys out in a basket or box all the time. Dogs get bored easily and will not play with any of them and then the owners wonder why. Instead, put some of the toys away and rotate them so as to make them more exciting. If your dog has not seen them in a while they will seem new. This is why, as parents, many despise cleaning out old toys in their child's room. Even though the child may not have touched a toy in months, as soon as it is going to make its departure it becomes more valuable due to psychological reactance. Dogs function in the same way so start rotating those toys!

This happens with our dogs all the time. Most often I witness this with curious puppies who have yet to encounter a full roll of toilet paper or their human sister's Barbie dolls. Most puppy owners rightfully keep their puppies in a gated area for the first few months of their lives to teach boundaries and house training. This, in my opinion, is an optimal way to train puppies as they are not instinctively prepared to have free reign of the house. What is also occurring in this situation, though, is that the sweet little puppy is developing psychological reactance to the rest of the house. Watch what happens if little puppy Max gets past the baby gate in the kitchen. He takes off like a bat out of hell flying through the house like a child running into Toys R Us with a $1,000 gift card. It's all new! The smells, the sounds, Mom's shoes as a new chew toy! The novelty of the rest of the house and achieving what he has been kept from for months is too exhilarating. He goes flying and bouncing off the living room couches, grabs a book off the coffee table, and starts making toilet paper origami around the house. How do you avoid this from building up with your pups or adult dogs that may be isolated from certain areas in the house? Do it in a controlled, calm manner and make it fun - but according to your definition of fun, not theirs. After all, the canine definition of fun may do more harm than good to your decor. Make sure your dog is somewhat tired (after a walk or exercise is good) and then stock up with his favorite treats (something super delicious like little pieces of chicken or hot dogs). Walk him calmly on a leash from room to room asking for behaviors, like sit, or hand targeting which should then be rewarded. Absolutely let him sniff around to allow his curiosity to be satiated but if he begins getting emotionally aroused, give him a break and try again a little later. Do this frequently in small bursts so as to keep the novelty of the rest of the house to a minimum. Again, if he "can" have it, it will not be as frustrating and exciting.

Along the same lines is something called saturation. Saturation is what dogs and humans need to do in order to be able to focus on a certain task. If you take your dog to a new park, it can be challenging to get him to focus on you at first, even with his favorite toy or smelly cheese in his face. This is due to the all the new smells, sights, and sounds that he is experiencing. If I take my nine-year-old son, Jason, to a World Wrestling Entertainment event and he sees his favorite wrestler coming down the ramp to the ring as we walk into the arena, there is no way in the world I would ask him to give me the answer to a math problem. It is just too much to ask at that point. I have to wait until the excitement dies down a bit and he has taken everything in. Use this principle of saturation when working with your dog. If you want him to be calm and focus on you in a certain area, he will need to frequent that area regularly. You will notice each time that the area will become less exciting as it becomes "old news" so to speak. I use saturation whenever I work with my dog or a client's dog because I am not going to place unrealistic expectations on the dog. Let him "get it out of his system" first and then he will be able to focus much more on what I am asking of him. It works like a charm.

Dominance My Arse

There is no shortage of books, television shows, magazines, and trainers these days touting the benefits of being the "pack leader" or the "alpha" in your relationship with your dog. Don't let your dog go in the door in front of you because he is being dominant. Don't let your dog pull you because he is being dominant. Don't let your dog sit on a higher level than you because he is being dominant. Don't let your dog put his paw on you because he is being dominant.

Let me tell you this. Sierra sleeps in our bed and puts her paws all over me as she tries to kiss me and jump on me if I have not seen her after a vacation or trip away and she doesn't have a "dominant" bone in her body.

Dr. David Mech, a well-known research scientist, was the originator of the alpha wolf theory but has since debunked this very theory. Mech states, "One of the outdated pieces of information is the concept of the alpha wolf. 'Alpha' implies competing with others and becoming top dog by winning a contest or battle. However, most wolves who lead packs achieved their position simply by mating and producing pups, which then became their pack. In other words they are merely breeders, or parents, and that's all we call them today, the 'breeding male,' 'breeding female,' or the 'male parent,' 'female parent,' or the 'adult male,' 'adult female.' " (n.d.).

How then did the alpha theory and race for dominance move from the world of wolves into the dog arena? It most likely came about by the "thought process that dogs are descended from wolves. Wolves live in hierarchical packs in which the aggressive alpha male rules over everyone else. Therefore, humans need to dominate their pet dogs to get them to behave." (Miller, 2011). In actual fact, one does not need to "dominate" one's dog because, contrary to the beliefs still widely held by many, dogs are not constructing some master plan to take over the human race. What they are doing, however, is whatever works to get what they want. Newsflash, so do you! The problem occurs when owners teach their dogs to get what they desire by performing undesirable behaviors, such as jumping up or pulling. Dogs do what works. Every single thing a dog does from the second he wakes up to the second he goes to sleep is because it works to get him what he wants, whether it be food, play, affection, safety, etc.

Now, don't go thinking this is in any way different from how you function. People also do what works to get what they want. If something they do is positively reinforced, the behavior will most likely happen again and again. Positive reinforcement works for children in school - I have used it for 20 years with much success - and it works for employees and employers as I have also been on both ends of that equation. It is pure science that, when something positive is added to a situation, the behavior will increase in frequency. If your dog is doing something you like, praise him for goodness sake! Let him know you like it. It works with kids, husbands, wives, dogs and just about anyone else, so start doing more of it and watch what happens.

(Photo: holbox/shutterstock.com)

Punishing a dog does nothing to fix a behavior issue and can cause further fear and aggression to develop. This dog's fear is obvious by the way she is cowering on her back to try to escape the raised hand, her furrowed brow, raised paw (a gesture of uncertainty or appeasement), and tight, closed mouth.

I also use this in my marriage as it is far more effective than pointing out the negative and trying to force my husband into doing what I want him to. My husband loves to cook (yes, I am very lucky!) and I make sure I always praise his meals to make sure they keep coming. My husband is a culinary genius but is not the most outspoken man when it comes to expressing his emotions, so I have used positive reinforcement over the years for this and surprise, surprise, the sweet talk behavior has increased in frequency. If something is not transpiring the way I would like, instead of yelling or using put-downs, I will calmly explain what I don't like and tell him what I do want, along with continuing the reinforcement of the desired behavior (in this case, the compliments).

This is just as effective with dogs and I use it on a daily basis with Sierra and with my clients' dogs. If a dog does something I don't like, I, of course, cannot explain to them what didn't work. What I can do, however, is remove what the dog is trying to get, such as by walking away to remove the attention when he jumps on me. If a dog is jumping on me, his goal is to gain my attention. If I yell 'no' or push him down, I am engaging with him, thus reinforcing the behavior. It doesn't matter that I yelled or pushed him as, in his mind, he just got the attention he was aiming for. Instead, telling the dog what I DO expect is the best way to communicate to him. Before the dog jumps, I will cue him to sit and immediately reinforce that behavior. Reinforcing the sit repeatedly will increase the frequency of the sit while decreasing the frequency of the jumping.

When the Going Gets Tough

Most parents would not re-home their child, although I know many who have thought of it after a bad day! If the kids are fighting, it is usually dealt with by time-outs or some other consequence. Yes, I know what you are thinking. Kids cannot kill each other (well, sure they can, but for the purposes of this argument, they cannot). Dogs who are fighting, however, can surely cause a lot of damage to both family members and each other. In cases like this, where safety is a concern and family members or dogs are thought to be in immediate danger, the advice of a skilled professional is key to see whether behavior modification or management are viable options. Sometimes, small tweaks to daily life can make all the difference with a dog that is struggling. Ultimately, re-homing may be a good choice for all humans and dogs involved.

A qualified canine behavior consultant can guide an owner to see what, why, and how the struggle is occurring and put a plan into place to get things on the right path before they get even worse. You are certainly not a bad owner for getting help. On the contrary. Be proud of yourself for taking the steps to improve your situation. I regularly hear from owners who call me for training that they have had dogs forever and should be able to fix whatever problem they are experiencing but no person is identical to another and dogs are different too. Do not feel badly about yourself if you feel like you are struggling and need to reach out for help. Enlisting the help of a qualified professional trainer and behavior consultant is one of the best and most honorable actions you can take as a pet owner.

Chapter 4

Putting the Safety Similarities to Use in Training

Safety, in my opinion, is equally, if not more important than physiological needs. As I described earlier with my rollercoaster example, fear can cause complete shut-down in humans and animals and MUST be addressed in order to decrease the intensity of the response. The number of behavioral issues that are caused by fear, and dog owners' unknowing contribution to these is disheartening. However, the more dog owners understand how fear works, the more they will be able to help their pets make a turnaround.

Potential behavior issues can begin even before a baby or puppy makes his or her appearance on the planet. What happens in utero can have a large impact on future behavior. Let's discuss babies first. Fetal alcohol syndrome, caused by excessive prenatal drinking, and crack baby syndrome, caused by smoking crack while pregnant, are examples of two diseases that can cause irreversible physical and mental harm to a baby. Further, research leans toward a high degree of stress during a mother's pregnancy causing long-term damage to a growing fetus. At the University of Denver, researchers Elysia Poggi Davis and Pilyoung Kim are focused not only on the environment of a child once he or she is born, but the external environment of the mother while the baby is in the womb. They determined that babies who are exposed to stress hormones (cortisol, for example) in utero can be affected long-term. (Davis, Glynn, Waffarn, & Sandman, 2011).

Davis (2011) published a study in *The Journal of Child Psychology and Psychiatry* in which she took 116 women and tested their levels of cortisol throughout their pregnancies. Testing occurred every month throughout the second and third trimesters. Once the babies were born, researchers took a blood draw from each baby's foot and measured the level of cortisol and also noted the babies' response to the blood draw. Researchers found that the greater the exposure to the mother's cortisol in the womb, the larger was the infants' cortisol spike in response to a blood draw in the first day of life. In addition, these babies were not able to calm down as easily after the blood draw. (Davis et al., 2011).

Tests also showed a higher level of cortisol-exposed babies in low-income environments. "If poor parents are working multiple jobs, if they have chronic shortages of resources, if they're trying to patch together low-wage jobs, government benefits, help from friends and family and neighbors, just the job of managing all that is a tremendous source of stress and anxiety for parents," says Philip Cohen, a sociologist at the University of Maryland. (Cohen (n.d.) cited in Pappas (2014)).

As shown in these studies and others of a similar nature, it is most beneficial for stress to be kept at a minimum during pregnancy. This is the same when it comes to dogs and is precisely why backyard breeding, puppy mills, and puppy stores need to go. Puppies bred and raised in horrific conditions such as puppy mills are not beginning their lives in an ideal situation, or one that is setting them up for any sort of success in the future. Many of these dogs live in cramped, filthy, abhorrent conditions and receive no socialization whatsoever with people or other dogs. The dogs and puppies are confined on a daily basis and receive little or no veterinary care, which is the reason so many are sick for months when they are brought to their new homes. The female mother dogs, meanwhile, are stressed, overbred, and often killed when they can no longer produce litters. The puppies do not spend adequate time with their mothers or siblings, and thus do not learn the lessons necessary for a productive and well-socialized life.

If a puppy store informs you that they get their dogs from "breeders," DO NOT BELIEVE THEM. Any reputable breeder will not sell their precious dogs to a store to sit in a cage all day. Instead, these puppies were, in most cases, in utero of a mother who was stressed on a daily basis and this does not bode well for a puppy's future. I know there are some dogs who have come from puppy stores and done really well. As with anything there are always exceptions to the rule. The nurture part of nature versus nurture can also come to play here and may help improve behavior, but a lot of puppies that have come from a stressed mother in an undesirable breeding environment are susceptible to having behavioral issues of some sort.

(Photo: KITSANANAN/Shutterstock.com)

Puppy mill puppies spend their days in cages with little to no outside interaction.

There have been many studies conducted on different species of animals regarding stress in utero. The effects on babies who were born to mothers who experienced psychological stress have been well studied in laboratory rodents, according to Hekman (2014). "When pregnant rats are subjected to acute stressors (such as restraint in a clear plastic tube for an hour a day), their offspring grow up to be less resilient to stress themselves," states Hekman. In addition, rats birthed from mothers who were stressed during pregnancy tend to have over-reactive stress systems. They have higher cortisol levels, have cortisol levels that rise more due to stress and take a longer time to decrease as opposed to rats born to mothers who were not stressed. Essentially, these fearful rats "have a stress system that is tuned higher, as if they are prepared for stressful events that never come." (Hekman, 2014).

Do you sometimes wonder why your dog is afraid of certain things that make no sense to you? Is he afraid of new things or environments? Perhaps as a pup he was not socialized properly, but research continues to show that animals exposed to elevated stress in the womb will be affected by it in some way after birth.

After birth, a child's or puppy's beginning of life experiences and enrichment definitely affect development and learning capabilities throughout life. A child who is exposed to more culture and positive experiences will, in many cases, become more well-rounded and knowledgeable. The same goes for puppies, which is why the socialization period is critical in giving puppies positive experiences to set them up for success - and the earlier the better. Exposures to violence, on the other hand, can cause social problems later in life. The US National Library of Medicine and National Institutes of Health states that a child witness of domestic violence is at risk for developing post-traumatic stress disorder that can result in permanent personality changes along with affecting his or her ability to effectively function in society as an adult (Tsavoussis, Stawicki, Stoicea, & Papadimos, 2014). Again, this is comparable in dogs. Negative experiences when young can affect a dog long-term. I am not saying dogs cannot improve with behavior modification and other tools, but the damage remains. Young dogs that are raised to fight may find it extremely difficult to live harmoniously among other dogs, although there will be exceptions. Many dogs or puppies that have been beaten or "disciplined" in a threatening way can develop deep-seated fears and aggression toward their owners or others.

What Do You Expect? I'm Just a Dog!

Let's discuss some easy changes owners can make to improve their understanding of their dogs' behavior. This will make interacting with them a little easier and, thus, more rewarding. It amazes me the high and sometimes ridiculous expectations people have for their dogs, when they would never set such high standards for children or other family members. Some owners seem to think that puppies come into this world speaking the owner's language (English, Spanish, pick your own), knowing how to walk on a leash (which to puppies and some dogs is just a swinging chew and tug toy), knowing that they are supposed to pee or poop in a certain spot, and the list continues. We would never expect a baby to immediately poop in the toilet without patiently guiding them once they are ready to do so. We would not scream at our developing child or someone learning a new language because they could not understand what we are attempting to communicate. We certainly do not expect our babies to hop off the hospital room table and start walking down the hall the minute they are born. But for some reason so many owners expect a totally different species, one that they have graciously brought into their homes, to do many of these things immediately. Never mind that they have not taken the time to guide or teach the dog what to do and how to do it, they get angry and frustrated when the dog does not respond "correctly." I am all for setting high standards in life but I certainly wouldn't have expected my son Jason, my future attorney, to come out of the womb and start arguing with me like he is so good at now. That took a lot of time, learning, and guidance.

Babies and children come into our lives and one of the first things parents do is baby-proof the home. Why do we do this? Because we are setting our child up for success, keeping him safe, and because he simply does not know any better. Children do not instinctively know what is expected so it is OUR job to teach them and show them.

Dogs come into our houses, many of them still puppies, and see a world of excitement and fun. An open square or rounded thing (aka a garbage can) with used food and wrappers that he gets to knock over, rummage around in and eat the best bits?? What could be better! Sometimes the humans even leave it open for him so he can just dig in - how nice of them! Oh, look, a nice, soft carpet that he can deposit his urine on so he does not have to go out in the cold - humans are so thoughtful! A hard square chew toy with numbered buttons on it that just happens to ring sometimes - that looks fun to gnaw on for a while. Your pup will love you for leaving all these cool things around for him. Getting my point? We MUST set our dogs up for success, just as we would our children as they learn what is expected. Use management to your advantage while your dog is learning the rules of your house and afterwards too, if necessary. For example, close the garbage can or put it in another room. Leaving a huge shoe rack out with 20 pairs of shoes and sneakers on it makes life easier for the family but is asking for trouble with a new puppy in the house. I certainly would not hesitate to utilize outlet covers when a baby is present. Is it irritating if I want to quickly use the outlet for something? Sure, but I know the baby is learning what is off-limits and I am avoiding potential mishaps and failures.

(Photo: Iko/shutterstock.com)

Provide your dog with plenty to do so your shoes don't become the most exciting thing to play with.

My dog Sierra was 2½ -3 years old when she joined our family. She had been found wandering the streets so we were clueless as to what she knew in terms of living in a house. I treated her like a puppy who was learning everything for the first time. This means that she was crated overnight and whenever we were not home so she did not have the opportunity to destroy things in the house. I did not leave food on the counters so she did not get the opportunity to become the next counter-surfing champion. I close my closets now too. I forgot once and quickly learned she liked to help herself to my boots and proudly prance around the house with them dangling from her mouth, although it was pretty damn cute to watch. It is my responsibility to take care of these things, not hers. My job is to set her up for success and that is what every dog needs.

I know what you're thinking. What do I do when my dog does something I don't like? Well, just like my getting a $250 speeding ticket years ago forced me to drive slower from then on, dogs need clear rules and consequences too. Would I still be driving slower if the cop, instead of just giving me a ticket had pulled me over and verbally and physically assaulted me? Most definitely. BUT, I also would be deathly afraid of any cops or getting stopped by anyone and an experience like that would have caused irreparable harm to me. Both consequences (the ticket or the verbal/physical assault) would stop the undesirable behavior, but the latter would cause long-term damaging effects to my psyche.

This is exactly how dogs learn as well. As owners and trainers, it is our duty to show them what is expected in a way that will not cause fear. It is our job to keep them feeling safe at all times, just as we would do for our children or spouses. Once fear has entered into the equation things become more problematic for all involved since it incites many unpredictable behaviors in humans and most certainly dogs too. What do I do if my new dog pees on the floor (which Sierra did quite a number of times in the beginning)? Do I yell at her, scream 'no,' and rub her nose in it? That will not teach her anything but to fear me and my ego does not necessitate that. What I do, though, is smack myself in the head for not watching her more closely to see the signs she is giving for having to go to the bathroom.

Dogs that are not house-broken should NEVER be out of sight, as that is the precise time they will use your new Persian rug as a toilet. It is your fault, not theirs. Instead, we need to take them out more frequently, watch for their signs of having to eliminate, and never leave them unsupervised. This may mean using a hands-free leash around your waist so they stay with you, crating them, or putting them in a gated room with a nice chew toy so they have something to occupy their minds. At the same time, we need to reinforce the behavior we do want. Reward and praise when they do eliminate outdoors. If they go outside and do not eliminate, we bring them back inside after a short time and crate for 10 or 15 minutes then try again. By using good management, clear expectations, and reinforcement of the desired behavior, we are now speaking the dog's language and setting up an ideal learning environment. Will there be mistakes? Absolutely, on both the dog's and owner's parts, but that's okay. Just go with the flow, do your best and don't be too hard on yourself – or the dog.

If a child keeps saying, "Mom, mom, mom, mom, mom...," is he being dominant? Well, he is being something I cannot exactly write here, but he is actually doing what works. If this nagging behavior has worked in the past to acquire what is desired, it will continue and actually increase in frequency. If a dog is jumping on you and nipping, is he being dominant? As you already know my thoughts on dominance and the damage it can cause, you know the answer is no, he is not being dominant. What he is doing, however, is attempting to get your attention and the behavior has most likely worked in the past to do just that. Are you going to follow the old school rules and push him down, grab his muzzle, or utilize any of those other outdated methods of "fixing" a behavior problem? Well, you could and the behavior may stop. On the other hand, it may not stop at all because you are only telling him what NOT to do, along with creating fear in the process. Using such techniques may also encourage a scared dog to start becoming aggressive to protect himself. How is he supposed to know what IS expected?

Our job as parents, dog owners, teachers, principals, cops, bosses, or whatever field we are in, is to communicate clearly what we do want. This happens to work really well in relationships, also! If a dog jumps on me, I turn away and say nothing and make no eye contact. This is how a dog can learn from consequences. If he jumps and mouths and I DO give him attention (yes, yelling 'NO' is attention), he learns to continue the behavior because it achieved what he wanted (i.e. my attention). By consistently removing the attention after the jump or nip, which in the terminology of behavior is known as negative punishment, the dog will learn that the behavior is not working to get what he desires. This decreases the need to repeat the behavior, meaning half of my job is complete. Now that he knows what not to do, the crucial part of my plan is to show him clearly what I do expect, which is to sit or be calm. This means I must reinforce the behavior I desire. By using whatever the dog finds reinforcing (toys, affection, food, etc.), I will reinforce this behavior repeatedly until it becomes part of the dog's repertoire. THAT is how dogs learn scientifically and most effectively.

When attempting to extinguish an undesirable behavior, humans and dogs can go through a highly frustrating part of the process known as an extinction burst. An extinction burst "refers to the concept of eliminating a behavior by refusing to reinforce it." (Williams, n.d). Pretend you take your daughter to a grocery store and each time you purchase a candy bar for her upon entering the store. After a while, you decide you do not want to buy the candy bar anymore and you tell your daughter 'no' when she asks for it. She begins to whine which causes you to once more buy the candy for her. Next time, you decide you have had enough and do not want to spend money on candy any more and will not buy it. She starts to cry and throw a temper tantrum. She throws a temper tantrum the second, third, and fourth time after you say no, also. By the fifth and sixth time, the behavior has diminished to whining opposed to a full-blown temper tantrum. Upon entering the store for the seventh time, your daughter has accepted the fact that no candy is coming and the whining no longer occurs. Your daughter's "temporary increase in whining when you decided to stop purchasing her chocolate candy bars is an example of extinction burst." (Williams, n.d.).

This is exactly what happens when an owner wants to stop giving in to a dog's demanding barking or pawing, for example. Any behavior that has previously been reinforced will go through extinction bursts and, for most owners, this can be a very trying time. Accepting that the behavior will get worse before it gets better (and it is the same with humans) and knowing that, if you stick with it, the behavior will stop are two things to think about to assist you in not pulling your hair out.

On the topic of frustration, there will come a period when dogs and humans like to relentlessly test their limits. Also known as adolescence, this period can be extremely frustrating for parents, teachers, dog owners or anyone who has to come in contact with said human or canine. Child adolescence occurs somewhere between the ages of 10-19, according to the World Health Organization. For dogs, adolescence begins around six months and continues until approximately 18 months. This can be a very disheartening period for owners and unfortunately, instead of hanging in there, many people relinquish their dogs to shelters during this period. During this tough time, I highly suggest going back to square one with your dog and tightening up the reins. Make sure the dog is earning everything he wants. Have him earn a fetch game but only after he sits and stays. Feed him only if he gives you full eye contact and exhibits impulse control while the bowl is being placed in front of him, meaning he should sit and stay until the bowl has been placed on the floor and you have given him a release cue, such as "okay!" to begin eating. I receive many calls from adolescent dog owners who, once the training is complete, are so relieved that they did not give up on their dogs. It can be a tough time but hang in there, as it will get better as long as you stick to being consistent, clear, and speaking a language your dog can understand.

Please Protect Me as You Would a Family Member

I know countless dogs that do not enjoy being approached, handled, or petted by strangers. In spite of this there is some unspoken rule, rigidly adhered to by many, that a dog must be petted when out and about. It often happens with someone who is "good with dogs," or who insists "dogs love me." Please, please, please be an advocate for your dog and his safety. I would never, as a mother, allow a stranger to come up and start handling my son, but for some odd reason well-meaning strangers feel it is acceptable to come toward someone with a dog and get down in his face, touch him, and goodness knows what else. This is so unfortunate for the dog as he may be anxiety-ridden but undergoing training to learn how to be more comfortable around people. Yet this invader has just put him over threshold. Humans can be arrested for behaving like this to each other but in the world of dogs it is almost considered rude if you **don't** allow someone to encroach on your dog's personal space. Don't feel bad about standing up for your dog. You can always say, "She has fleas!" or something similar. That usually will do the job for most "good with dogs" strangers.

Another inconsistency concerning safety among dogs and humans is how each species is looked upon when forced to protect themselves. We hear stories in the news all the time of human heroes who defended themselves from someone who was attempting to cause them bodily harm, which is understandably viewed as justified. Why should this be any different when it comes to dogs? I am not talking about dogs who bite for any other reason than being forced to protect their own well-being or a human or animal in danger. We should not and cannot blame dogs who protect themselves from being mistreated, poked, or prodded. They have most likely given many warning signs that were not acknowledged or respected. People must either educate themselves or not take it upon themselves to do whatever they choose to a dog. Go to *YouTube* and type in "dog bites news reporter" and watch closely. The humans are completely at fault for the biting incidents. No one should EVER hold or get that close to an unfamiliar dog's face. Dogs – including the ones in the many videos freely available - usually give many warning signs. These include freezing in place, "whale eye" (i.e. looking out of the sides of their eyes and showing the whites of the eyes), ears back, and a furrowed brow. This all goes along with what I discussed in the last paragraph. Why should it be acceptable for a stranger to kneel down and grab a dog by the head and expect nothing unfortunate to happen? You would never see that on the news with a reporter and a child because it simply would not be accepted. It is something we just don't do. It is high time we apply this to dogs too because, according to *DogsBite.org*, the number of dog bites continues to rise. In many cases these occurrences could have been avoided if people used the same rules for human interactions as they do in their interactions with dogs.

The second level of Maslow's *Hierarchy of Needs*, which is the safety level, cannot be overlooked here. It is key that dogs feel safe. If they do not, problems will usually arise in some form or another. Dogs too experience fear, stress, and many other feelings that humans encounter in similar situations. There is good stress, such as a wedding, a new job, a new baby, or a move to a new house. These are all exciting times but can also create stress for the people and pets involved. I know that when I experienced my wedding, a job change, or a move I was ecstatic yet also out of sorts for a while. When I moved into my most recent home, my Doberman, Pharaoh (RIP) started acting quite strangely for a dog of seven years of age. He started pacing, urinating in the house, licking the carpet, and engaging in some other odd behaviors too. I knew it had to be the upheaval of the move so I immediately got his mind active. I increased his exercise and implemented more mentally stimulating activities for him, such as feeding him out of interactive feeding toys instead of out of a bowl. I also played soft, classical music which research has shown to sometimes help calm dogs. After a few days and increasing these activities, he started to settle in and bounce back to his old self.

Dogs cannot communicate verbally when they are stressed but their emotions will most likely be depicted in their behavior. Listen to what they tell you and help them through the stressful times as best you can. As previously mentioned, fear in humans and dogs can cause complete shut-down and renders learning virtually impossible. Fear is best dealt with the same way in dogs as it is in humans. Unfortunately, fallacies that fear should not be reinforced, or that attempting to comfort a fearful human or dog will backfire and increase the fear, are common. This could not be further from the truth. Fear is an emotion and not a behavior. You cannot reinforce emotions. If my son wakes up from a nightmare and is scared, yelling at him or forcing him back to bed without any comforting is not going to make the fear dissipate. It is more likely to increase the fear and leave him feeling abandoned. On the other hand, sitting with him for a few minutes and rubbing his back works wonders in reducing his fear and helping him get back to sleep. Soothing a dog during a thunderstorm is not going to make the fearful behavior increase. Rather, it will show him that he is not alone and the comfort he needs will be provided to help him through the storm.

To further explain this, behavioral researchers in the 1940s conditioned rats to jump to the other side of their enclosure to avoid an electric shock that followed the sound of a buzzer. In the next phase of training, the researchers changed the sequence so that cheese followed the buzzer and the shock was discontinued.

Over multiple experiences with cheese following the buzzer, even as the rats attempted to jump to the other side, do you think the rats became more fearful and increased their jumping behavior? That is what would happen if you believe the jumping behavior (and therefore the fear) was reinforced by the cheese. Just the opposite occurred. The rats' fear decreased, the jumping stopped and they began to eat the cheese. This is an example of "classical conditioning changing behavior by changing emotional state rather than operant conditioning rewarding fear." (Hetts & Estep, 2007).

It is critical that our dogs, as well as the humans in our lives, feel safe in order to successfully advance along the *Hierarchy of Needs* toward self-actualization. If a dog is afraid of something, it must be dealt with through care, comforting, and behavior modification. Dogs should never be forced to "get used to" a stimulus that they find frightening or threatening. In most cases, this does not happen. Instead, the fear becomes worse because of the overwhelming reaction to being "flooded" with what scares them. Flooding means forcing an animal into a situation which causes fear in an attempt to make him "get used to it."

Using the scientific method of desensitization and counterconditioning, dogs and humans can slowly learn to change their emotional responses to their fears. If I am afraid of mice, tossing me in a room with large mice furiously scampering around on the floor and walls would be flooding and would in no way, shape, or form help me "get used to" them. Rather, it would have the opposite effect of making me more frightened than when I began. Slowly introducing me to tiny mice in a glass case where I can decide how close I get would be a good first step in addressing my fear. When I was on the scary upside down, twisty rollercoaster it was also "flooding." Starting out on a much smaller rollercoaster would have been a good way to begin desensitizing me to the experience.

If a dog is afraid of other dogs, for example, dragging him on leash right up to another dog and "correcting" him for barking, lunging, or other behavior deemed unacceptable is not an ideal way to remedy the behavior. Putting the dog over threshold like this does not fix anything. Instead, the dog must begin at a distance that elicits no reaction. Here and only here is where the desensitization and counterconditioning can scientifically and effectively work.

When a human or canine is not fond of or afraid of something, they have developed what is called a negative conditioned emotional response (abbreviated as -CER) and these can be experienced through any sense (touch, smell, hearing, taste, or sight). The term conditioned emotional response (CER) means a "learned emotional reaction like anxiety or happiness that occurs as a response to predictive cues." (Dewey, 2007). This happens frequently to us as humans and we don't even realize that is what we are experiencing. One of my favorite TV shows is *King of Queens*, starring Kevin James and Leah Remini. I have seen pretty much every episode but one of my favorites of all time involves Kevin James' character, Doug Heffernan, making a feeble attempt to get his wife, Carrie, to take a pole dancing class. After a lot of persuasion, Carrie decides to give it a try. Surprisingly, she becomes addicted to it and wants nothing more than to dance for her husband each day. Unfortunately, for Doug, Carrie is absolutely terrible and has no pole dancing skills to speak of even after a great deal of practice. Carrie's excitement for the dancing prompts her to print coupons for Doug to use each night for a free dance. At one point in the episode Carrie presents Doug with a stack of additional coupons to use and he finally blows a gasket and tells her how horrendous a dancer she is. The thought of Carrie dancing for him once provided Doug a very positive CER, but now he tells Carrie that the mere sight of the coupons sends shivers through his body, and not in the way he had hoped. The coupons have taken on a very negative meaning and developed a negative CER for Doug.

Take out a leash and see your dog bounce off the walls with excitement. Is your dog getting that thrilled over a six foot piece of nylon? No, it is what the leash predicts that causes the elation. Now, take out nail clippers for a dog that does not enjoy having his paws touched. The dog may run away, cower into a corner, shake, or exhibit a variety of other fearful behaviors. These are examples of positive and negative conditioned emotional responses. Here is another: I despise my alarm clock. I am not a morning person so when that alarm clock rings at the crack of dawn, I get a feeling of overwhelming dread throughout my body.

If I happen to set that same alarm clock during the day for some reason, the same feeling of dread comes over me when I hear it. Sometimes I will choose a new alarm sound until that one develops the same negative CER that the original one produced. One day (in my dreams), my alarm clock rings and the bedroom door bursts open with my husband lovingly presenting me with a wonderful buffet breakfast and $1,000 to spend however I wish.

This continues to happen daily for a while and, over a period of time, I start to notice that I am actually looking forward to that alarm clock going off as I am now wondering all different sorts of fun things. What will the breakfast be today? Something new and delicious? Where will I spend the $1,000? Will I spend it all in one place? My feelings and emotions about that terrible sound are now changing to excitement, anticipation, and fun!

You can use this information to understand what type of feelings your dog may be experiencing as you go through life exactly the same way.

Human -CERs:

> Hearing a dentist's drill (because it predicts getting a cavity filled).
> Hearing the UPS truck (because it predicts the dog will react in an undesirable way).
> Smelling a certain cologne/perfume (because it predicts someone you dislike being close).

Canine -CERs:

> Driving into the parking lot at the veterinarian's office (because it predicts pain and being uncomfortable).
> Hearing the UPS truck (because it predicts a uniformed stranger is approaching the house).
> Seeing nail clippers (because it predicts being uncomfortable).

Human +CERs:

> Smelling sunblock (because it predicts the fun of summer).
> Hearing the car door close when a loved one gets home at the end of the day (because it predicts being close to someone you love).

Canine +CERs:

> Seeing the owner pick up a leash for a walk (because it predicts going outside to smell amazing scents and get fresh air).
> Someone opening a certain cabinet because the treats are kept inside (because it predicts eating yummy food).
> Hearing a Ziploc bag crinkle (because it predicts eating yummy food).
> Hearing the owner's car pulling into the driveway (because it predicts seeing a loved family member).

Your dog is experiencing many of these feelings just like you are. Be mindful when you feel as if you want to push him into doing something he is uncomfortable with or when he seems afraid. Put yourself in his shoes and think how you would best benefit from the situation. It is not much different at all.

Give Me Structure!

Most humans, like canines, thrive on routine and structure and can feel out of sorts when their trusted routine gets shaken up. Security and stability are two very integral parts of the safety rung on Maslow's *Hierarchy of Needs*. Most humans or canines cannot and will not function well or at their highest potential if these two significant factors are missing from their lives.

Consistency and resiliency can be grouped into the safety level on the *Hierarchy of Needs* and both of these are critical to human and canine success. Consistency provides clarity and understanding and this is a must in human and canine learning. In

all my years of teaching, students who had had the most consistency at home had an easier time in school. In all my years of dog training, it was just the same. My doggy parent clients that provided the most consistency and structure for their dogs overall had the most well-behaved dogs. In response to the question, 'Why is consistency important?' the University of Alabama Child Development Resources states the following:
"Consistency gives a child a sense of security. They learn they can rely on their parents and trust that their needs will be met. This helps in the bonding process." (n.d.).

The report states:

> ➤ Children with consistent parents experience less anxiety.
> ➤ Developing a daily routine with regular rising times, bedtimes, after school schedules, and meal times will cultivate a more peaceful home life.
> ➤ Consistency helps children develop a sense of responsibility because they know what their parents expect from them.
> ➤ Children who have consistent rules with predictable consequences are less likely to "push the limits" and constantly test their parents by misbehaving. They learn quickly that "no" means "no."
> ➤ Investing early in consistent parenting pays off huge dividends later. There will be considerably fewer temper tantrums, arguing and bargaining as the children grow.
> ➤ Without consistency children must "guess" daily what actions are appropriate. They wonder if everything that takes place happens because they did something to make it happen.
> ➤ Inconsistent parenting causes confusion, poor self-esteem and oftentimes very negative values.

(University of Alabama, n.d.)

This information applies to adults as well, especially in the workplace. My most respected bosses over the years were the ones that treated their staff using the above principles. When we know what to expect as humans, life becomes much less complicated. Go back and read the list again and this time, think of your dog and ask yourself if you are providing those things for him. Every single one of the above applies to dogs and their level of success as members of our families. We humans desire consistency and thrive with it, and so do our dogs. It is our responsibility to provide it for them just as we would for our families. It will only simplify our lives as dog owners.

In my teaching days, I remember feeling sympathy for some students who came from divorced parents (as does my son, Jason). This was not because they were treated poorly or for any other reason besides the fact that some of them struggled with a lack of consistency caused by going back and forth between two homes. Most children were resilient enough to handle it with minimal issues, but some did battle a little and had a difficult time remembering to bring certain things to school, for example. In the event I sent materials home or emailed parents, I would ensure that I covered both bases and both parents received the information to keep consistency at the forefront for the child. This is yet another parallelism to the canine world as I have had a couple clients who "share" a dog so the dog splits time 50/50 at each house. For a puppy, this can be terribly difficult, especially one who is learning housebreaking, rules, and boundaries. Consistency is key and is paramount to success with humans and dogs. The owners would wonder why behavior was not ideal and in most cases, consistency – or the lack of it - is the reason.

Another discernible likeness between dogs and humans is resiliency and personality/temperament. Every child or adult has his or her own personality. It is not unlikely to see two siblings from the same parents be a far cry from each other in terms of personality, as is the case in my family and innumerable others. One child from a family can be independent, resilient, hard-working, dedicated, and philanthropic while a sibling can be the disastrous opposite. Is it nature or nurture or a combination of both? This is hard for many dog owners to understand when their loyal and sweet 13-year-old golden retriever, Max, passes away and they wind up with a golden retriever puppy who is nothing like the "perfect" dog that has passed. "Max never left our side and we could have him off leash and he would always come back. He never mouthed us like this new dog does. This new pup is crazy!" they might say. Well, I do believe that dogs can be drastically diverse, but I also believe many people forget how their little angels behaved 15 years prior as puppies. I have yet to meet a puppy that does not put those razor sharp teeth on any skin he can get his mouth on!

Some dogs are very independent, either due to their breed or because that is "just the way they are." Humans have identical traits. Some dogs will not leave your side to the extent that you might think you have gained a Siamese twin. I happen to think that the kinder we are to our dogs, the more they tend to want to be near us more. But it goes deeper than that. There are certain owners who express their frustration that a previous dog would not leave their side and relied on the owner for their every move. Now, however, they have this independent, "stubborn" dog that will not come when called or follow them anywhere. I see this as clear as day when I am pet sitting dogs in my own home. I have had three dogs staying at once and they all enter my home differently and behave just like you would expect kids or adults to behave when meeting new people. You have your outgoing personality who walks around like he owns the joint. You have the shy one who is timid about meeting the new dogs and keeps to herself. You have the one who adapts very easily and acts as if she has been living there for years. These "personalities" are exactly what you would see at a party with humans. At a social gathering you will see the "life of the party," who is comfortably surrounded by many partygoers. In contrast to that, there will most likely be a wallflower or two, and then plenty in between. Compare this also to a dog park setting as you will witness the exact same dynamics there. You will have the very social dogs, the bully dogs, the dogs hanging by their owners, the dogs hiding under the benches, and many in between.

I would like to address the bully dog, or, as some like to say, the "dominant" dog, although I do my best to leave that word out of my vocabulary. You can customarily find a bully dog in a dog park or doggy daycare on any given day. You know, the one that likes to pin other dogs down, is ready to pounce at the gate when a new dog is entering, and just seems to lack the social skills that we would like to see in our canine friends. Many of these bully dogs lacked the early experiences of learning how to behave around other dogs, due to lack of positive socialization with other dogs or owners who did not take the time to train them. Most of these cases can be fixed between the dogs themselves as many will do a good job of putting the bully dog in his place. If the behavior is not dealt with, however, bullying can become self-reinforcing and increase in frequency, duration, and magnitude. It is essential that owners are aware that they need to intercede if a victim dog is scared or is not able (or confident enough) to teach the bully how to act properly.

A consent test is a very effective tool to use if there is uncertainty about the motives of a dog. Keep the "bully" dog in one place and, if the playmate runs away, you have your answer. If the play partner hangs around and tries to continue the play, she has let you know she is fine with the interaction. Think of this as the equivalent of the victim dog saying 'yes' or 'no.' Bully dogs, in my opinion, should not frequent dog parks because of the myriad of issues that may arise. Removing the bully from the situation each time an incident occurs is a good way to decrease the behavior. Many owners will scold or hit their dog for bullying behavior, but that is neither necessary nor effective long-term. This only serves to scare a dog and may cause fear and aggression issues which are much more difficult to fix than simply doing time-outs or calling the dog away and rewarding him for coming to you. You can also take away the reward (i.e. access to other dogs in the dog park) each time an incident occurs and see what happens then. Remember, according to the science of behavior, consistently removing a positive reward when a negative behavior occurs will make the undesirable behavior decrease.

Human bullies function in an identical manner and should be dealt with similarly. Child and adult bullies "get off" on the feeling of power and being in control and may have been bullied themselves in the past. In many instances, when a person steps up to a bully and puts him in his place either verbally or physically, things start to change for the better. Most bullies tend to pick on the weak and those they think will not fight back so when a counterattack does ensue, they may back down. If your dog or child or co-worker is a bully, don't sit back and watch. Step up, get involved, and stop the bullying from going any further. If more people lived their lives this way, there would be fewer fights at dog parks and fewer troubles in life in general.

(Photo: Sheeva1/Shutterstock.com)

The dog on the right is bullying the other dog. The bully dog's body language includes a very forward posture that pushes the other dog back as well as raised lips to bare the teeth.

Fear-Free Vets

Dr. Marty Becker, a world-renowned American veterinarian, has recently launched an initiative for "fear-free" veterinary offices. How many of your dogs shut down or act out during a visit to the vet? Many dogs shake uncontrollably, drool, pace, lunge, bark, and engage in many other unwanted behaviors when walking into a vet's office. As we know, many have developed a very negative CER to the situation because they know what lies ahead. Dr. Becker has proposed such changes as playing classical music in veterinary clinics, which research has shown to assist in calming some dogs (Kogan, Schoenfeld-Tacher, & Simon, 2012). He has suggested having a "big treat budget," offering treats ranging from Easy Cheese to hot dogs to help dogs form a stronger positive CER to the office. Changing the outdated buzzing fluorescent lights, switching to yoga mats on the floor as opposed to cold, hard, high exam tables, and changing the paint colors on the walls are some of the innovative ideas behind this initiative. When we take children to the pediatrician, the offices usually have toys, brightly colored paintings, fish tanks, and other fun items to keep the mood happy and calm for children. We know that dogs can benefit just as much from this, so I am absolutely ecstatic with the forward thinking of this fear-free movement and I know all of our dogs will be as well.

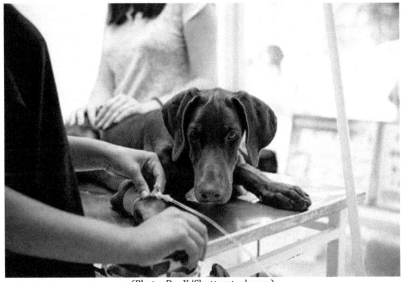

(Photo: DuxX/Shutterstock.com)

This dog is showing signs of anxiety while being examined at the vet and getting an IV placed. Some of these signs include a tense body posture, furrowed brow, and tight closed mouth.

(Photo: Dmitri Ma/Shutterstock.com)

Fear-free vets are the way of the future. This dog is clearly showing signs of being relaxed and having fun. Some of these signs include loose and jiggly body, relaxed open mouth, and ears in natural position. Examining dogs on the floor as opposed to cold, hard tables is one thing that renowned veterinarian Dr. Marty Becker is proposing to help make the veterinary experience better for dogs.

"Once pets know fear and anxiety and stress, you can't undo it," Becker says. "You can see it. You can smell it because dogs are stained with their own saliva from licking themselves. You can hear it and feel it." (Becker (n.d.) cited in Manning (2016)).

Stress and fear can lead animals to hide the symptoms that prompted the vet visit, and may even alter their test results, says

Richard A. LeCouteur, a veterinarian with a specialty in neurology and a professor emeritus at the University of California at Davis' School of Veterinary Medicine. Dr. John Talmadge, meanwhile, says the fear-free approach is proving popular. "We have more than doubled our business through [the Bigger Road Veterinary Center in Springboro, Ohio] since opening (in April) and are well ahead of where we thought we would be," he says (Talmadge (n.d.) cited in Manning (2016)).

Chapter 5

Putting the Love and Belonging Similarities to Use in Training

Continuing with Maslow's *Hierarchy of Needs*, the next level features love and belonging. This is where many of us, as dog owners, tend to dive in pretty heavily and spoil our dogs. Good for us! They are here to be spoiled and that is just what I do. My dog Sierra is treated like a member of our family and she is one happy dog. She sleeps in bed with us (no, it won't make her "dominant"), she cuddles on the couch with us (no, it won't make her "dominant") and she is included in as many family activities as we can allow her to take part. What she does know, though, is that before she jumps up on the bed she has to sit and wait patiently until she is invited up. When people ask me if they should allow their dogs on the bed or couches, my answer is always the same. There is no right or wrong answer - it only matters what YOU as the owner want. The only time I would not recommend that a dog has the rights to furniture is if he begins to guard his space and will not get off willingly. In such cases, training needs to be implemented to get to the root of the problem and remedy the guarding issue. With help from a professional force-free trainer, an owner of a dog who guards a couch (or similar) can learn how to handle the issue without making it worse. A dog who is guarding something needs to be taught that it is more fun to relinquish it and that is exactly what a good trainer can aid with.

When I walk into someone's home for the first time to help train their dogs, it is generally quite easy to spot the dogs that receive heaps of love from their families. This is a point strangers and friends always make about my son, Jason and my dog, Sierra, i.e. that they seem so happy and must get a lot of love. They sure do and it shows! Humans function the same way as dogs. If we feel loved, most of us are inclined to give that love right back.

For years dog owners have proclaimed, "My dog loves me!!" and many trainers, although somewhat believing it themselves, would cringe at the statement because there was no scientific evidence to back it up. Research in the past few years, however, is starting to show evidence of what we knew deep down all along. Our dogs do love us! Gregory Berns (2013) states, "The ability to experience positive emotions, like love and attachment, would mean that dogs have a level of sentience comparable to that of a human child. And this ability suggests a rethinking of how we treat dogs."

I am so saddened by how frequently I hear or read about people who do not want to give their dogs "too much love or attention" because they will get "spoiled." Would we ever do this to our kids or spouses or friends? No, of course not! Why would holding back love be a good thing? We need it. We thrive on it and so do dogs.

Social psychologist and Stanford assistant professor, Gregory Walton states, "Belonging is a psychological lever that has broad consequences. Our interests, motivation, health and happiness are inextricably tied to the feeling that we belong to a greater community that may share common interests and aspirations. Isolation, loneliness and low social status can harm a person's subjective sense of well-being, as well as his or her intellectual achievement, immune function and health. Research shows that even a single instance of exclusion can undermine well-being, IQ test performance and self-control." (Walton (n.d.) cited in Enayati (2012)).

Walton's earlier studies demonstrate that a sense of social belonging can affect one's motivation and continued "sticktuitiveness," even on impossible tasks. That is, if you don't feel like you belong, you are both less motivated and more likely to quit in the face of obstacles.

Let's Be Friends

I would never run up to someone and stick my nose in their butt to say 'hello' and I would certainly hope you would agree. I would kindly say 'hi,' introduce myself and perhaps shake hands. If they were someone of whom I was not a fan, I assuredly would not lunge at them and scream profanities, although it might be a tempting proposition. Besides the initial greeting, humans and dogs feel and behave very similarly with their friends and families. Find me one pair of siblings that has never argued or had a fight. I don't think you can. It is almost expected for siblings, spouses, friends, and co-workers to have disagreements but, for some strange reason, many people believe that dogs should never have disagreements. Dogs have skirmishes over toys, bones, owners' affection, food, space on the couch, and anything else you can imagine. Yes, we worry because dogs are capable of causing irreparable harm so we tend to be a bit more "helicopter parent-y" than we would with our children, perhaps. If the doggy debates are not causing bodily injury and trips to the vet, let them work it out to a point where you feel comfortable. If you feel you cannot read the body language accurately, there is no harm in simply clapping, stomping feet, or loudly saying "okay!" to redirect them and give them a break. Most dogs will normally work out glitches in a relationship better than most humans. We can learn so much from them. If the skirmishes are regularly getting out of hand, however, consult a force-free behavior consultant for assistance.

Have you ever really thought about why humans will pay a large amount of money to sit in an arena and watch two other humans beat the hell out of each other? What is the draw? Studies have shown that mice and other animals are actually drawn to violence. Up until recently though, scientists did not quite know how the brain was actually involved. Then, a study in 2008, detailed in the journal *Psychopharmacology*, reveals the same clusters of brain cells involved in other rewards are also behind the craving for violence.

"Aggression occurs among virtually all vertebrates and is necessary to get and keep important resources such as mates, territory and food," says study team member Craig Kennedy, professor of special education and pediatrics at Vanderbilt University in Tennessee. "We have found that the reward pathway in the brain becomes engaged in response to an aggressive event and that dopamine is involved." (Couppis & Kennedy, 2008).

Kennedy explains that the experiments have implications for humans in that the reward pathways in the brains of humans and mice are very similar. "Aggression is highly conserved in vertebrates in general and particularly in mammals," Kennedy says. "Almost all mammals are aggressive in some way or another. It serves a really useful evolutionary role probably, which is you defend territory; you defend your mate; if you're a female, you defend your offspring." (Couppis & Kennedy, 2008).

Prof. Kennedy is absolutely right. I am definitely a Mama Bear when it comes my son.

Now before we completely lose hope in the human and canine races, as much as there is a propensity for violence, there is plenty for love and caring, as well. Watch two young children play together and note the sharing, kindness, and love that transfers between the two. (Yes, I know you parents are thinking I am nuts, but it does happen on occasion!) Watch two housemate dogs as they cuddle together. There is nothing more precious. Believe it or not, a very recent study has depicted dogs to be even kinder and gentler than we thought. A new study by researchers in Austria suggests that dogs are prosocial among their own kind too. The discovery was made via an experiment that involved the voluntary offering of food between dogs. The results showed that dogs also – perhaps surprisingly - grasp the concept of giving and sharing.

"Dogs and their nearest relatives, the wolves, exhibit social and cooperative behaviour, so there are grounds to assume that these animals also behave prosocially toward conspecifics," says Friederike Range, an ethologist at the Messerli Research Institute in Vienna, Austria. "Additionally, over thousands of years of domestication, dogs were selected for special social skills." (Range, Quervel-Chaumette, Dale, & Marshall-Pescini, 2015).

Range states that gathering and measuring information on prosocial behavior in dogs is a challenge because they are so social with humans. Researchers find it difficult to see the difference between prosocial behaviors and behaviors that may simply be dogs responding to cues from the researchers. To take people out of the equation as much as possible, Range and her colleagues conducted an experiment where two dogs were set up by themselves in cages side-by-side. One of the dogs, called the donor dog, had the ability to extend one of two trays toward a receiver dog, using his mouth to pull on a string. One of these trays contained a treat, while the other was empty. The dogs had been trained over weeks to understand how the tray-pulling system worked, and the donor dog in each instance knew he would receive nothing if he gave the treat to his fellow canine (other than the pleasure perhaps of knowing he had done a kindness to his counterpart). The researchers found that dogs, in the absence of any ulterior motive, do indeed exhibit prosocial behavior, in this case by voluntarily giving food to other dogs. But having said that, they can also be accused of preferential treatment.

"Dogs truly behave prosocially toward other dogs. That had never been experimentally demonstrated before," says Range. "What we also found was that the degree of familiarity among the dogs further influenced this behaviour. Prosocial behaviour was exhibited less frequently toward unfamiliar dogs than toward familiar ones." (Range et al., 2015).

In other words, "dogs look out for their friends more than they do random strangers, but the same could be said of our own prosocial behaviour. Humans have the capacity for kindness, but we demonstrate it more frequently with those with which we are more familiar." (Dockrill, 2015).

Body Language to Communicate

What are the differences between the two women in this picture?

(Photo: Antonio Guillem/Shutterstock.com)

Overbearing woman with a scared woman.

68

...and this picture?

(Photo: Rita Kochmarjova/Shutterstock.com)

Overbearing dog with a scared dog.

Besides the species involved, there are not many differences at all. You have one overbearing, angry individual becoming aggressive and one confused, scared individual on the other side. The aggressor in both cases is leaning into the body of the aggressee. Both aggressors are baring their teeth with their mouths wide open and have very tense body language that is pushing the aggressee back into a corner, figuratively. Both victims look frightened and are cowering away with fearful, wide eyes. Both aggressors are most likely trying to make a point about something, which we are not privy to.

Body language is very telling in humans but is even more so in canines, due to their lack of spoken language skills. Everything is conveyed through body language, facial expressions, and some general vocalizing. Carefully study two dogs that have never met before and see the extraordinary body movements and cues they present to each other. It is absolutely fascinating and, as a professional dog trainer, this is how much of our training is done. We are constantly listening to dogs via what they tell us with their body language. We can learn a great deal this way if we know how to really listen. Set a goal for yourself to learn more about what your dog tells you via his body language and facial expression. The communication and level of understanding as well as the bond between the two of you can benefit greatly from this knowledge. Dogs are craving for it. Yes, many people are aware of typical canine signals, such as backing away or growling when fearful or showing a doggy smile with loose body language when happy, but there are also many signals that people do not see, do not know about, or that are misunderstood. A little education could make life so much easier for all involved.

Many body language signs dogs use are exactly the same as humans. Some examples are:

> Fear – cowering, looking to the side, trembling, ears back, panting, pacing, lip licking, running to owner or parent, backing away.
> Anger/aggression – leaning forward, "in your face," yelling/barking, chest out and stiff body/tail up and stiff body.
> Playful – loose body, ears relaxed, jumping around, being "silly," play bow in dogs.

(Photo: cynoclub/Shutterstock.com)

A play bow is a meta signal that indicates to other dogs that all ensuing behavior has a playful intent.

70

(Photo: The Len/Shutterstock.com)

This dog is indicating that he does not want to be approached. The body language signs of this include baring teeth, tense mouth, "hard" staring eyes, dilated pupils, and leaning forward.

(Photo: InesBazdar/Shutterstock.com)

This man is indicating that he does not want to be approached. The body language signs of this include crossed arms, "hard" staring eyes, grimace, and tense body.

How do humans communicate to each other with body language or facial expressions? Seeing someone cross their arms is not the most inviting posture and, combined with a scowl, would make me think twice about approaching. On the other hand, observing a smiling, happy person with a loose body is very inviting and screams approachability. With dogs, a frozen, tight body paired with growling or teeth baring would be quite non-approachable, while a dog with a jiggly, loose body and a doggy "smile" means "come on over!" Most humans are well-versed in reading human body language as are many dogs and, of course, most dogs are adept at reading the many signals displayed by other dogs. The missing piece here is humans' ability to read dog body language, which is why there are so many unfortunate incidents between humans and dogs. It is critical to be able to hear what your dog is telling you so you can help him, just as you would your child, spouse, friend or family member.

Humans also mirror each other's body language and facial expressions. If someone is smiling, it is almost contagious and we tend to become a reflection of that other person. If someone is laughing, I know I find it difficult not to at least smile, but usually will laugh along with them. A very interesting study emerged recently that shows that dogs can actually imitate each other's expressions, just like humans do. In the past, this was only thought to be possible by humans and non-human primates, like chimpanzees or orangutans. Researchers from the Natural History Museum at the University of Pisa, Italy have determined that dogs' mirroring of facial expressions may have arisen during their domestication.

"We demonstrated that rapid mimicry is present in dogs and it is an involuntary, automatic and split-second mirroring of other dogs," says lead researcher Dr. Elisabetta Palagi in *Royal Society Open Science*. According to Dr. Palagi (2015), dogs are actually displaying a type of empathy in their ability to decipher the emotions of another dog through facial expressions and movements of the body. The dogs in the study were observed playing together in a park and were found to be able to mimic the facial expression of the dogs they were playing with in a millisecond. It was determined that this ability is completely reflex and not a result of training. (Palagi, Nicotra, & Cordoni, 2015).

Dr. John Bradshaw at the University of the Bristol School of Veterinary Science in England believes more research is needed to establish if dogs are really able to sense what emotions are at the forefront of other dogs' minds.

"Domestic dogs are exquisite readers of body language, both that of other dogs, and, uniquely, our own - which is why they're so easy to train. They also love to play, so quickly learn that imitating the actions of their play-partner means that the game goes on for longer but science has yet to show that dogs have any understanding of other dogs' thought-processes, or emotions," says Bradshaw. (Bradshaw (n.d.) cited in Turner, (2015)).

Dogs are known to be able to respond to human emotions, e.g. copying a yawn, suggesting they show some basic aspects of empathy. This capacity may have evolved in dogs as they were domesticated or could have already been present in the wild ancestors of canines.

Chapter 6

Putting the Esteem Similarities

to Use in Training

Fish Can't Climb Trees

Everybody is a genius, but if you judge a fish by its ability to climb a tree, it will live its whole life thinking that it is stupid. - Anonymous (n.d.)

Parents need to fill a child's bucket of self-esteem so high that the rest of the world can't poke enough holes to drain it dry. - Alvin Price (n.d.)

Our jobs as parents, teachers, coaches, and humans is to build others up, not break them down. Giving a compliment and seeing the smile on someone's face is priceless. Watching a child score his first basket in a game is priceless. Watching a dog figure out a puzzle toy is priceless. Why is it priceless? Because we know ourselves the feelings of accomplishment and joy that accompany each of them. My most influential teachers and coaches in the past were positive, encouraging, and helpful, and led me to believe I could reach the stars. Opposite experiences taught me a great deal as well and although I learned from those, my success was due solely to the positive experiences and being guided in a supportive manner. I will never forget those people because they drastically changed my life for the better.

As a teacher for a number of years, I have come across many teachers who build students up and, unfortunately, many who break them down. You can always observe the looks on the students' faces to decode what type of teacher they are experiencing. The more fun learning is, the more likely it is that the students will have a light in their eyes and be fully engaged. Engaged students are active and willing participants in the learning process. When students are not enjoying the process, they are more likely to look like robots who are simply going through the motions. I have heard music teachers in the past tell students they sound awful! Now, will that make students try harder? Perhaps, but talk about killing morale and a love for learning. That is undeniably the way to do it. The students may sound pleasing to the ear because they are petrified of making mistakes and disappointing the teacher, but what is that teaching them about how to live life? I want my students to not be afraid to take risks and to not be fearful of making mistakes because of the fallout. Mistakes are how we learn for goodness sake! I want my students (human and dog) to enjoy life and not live in fear. As was stated so beautifully by an unknown author, "When I was 5 years old, my mother always told me that happiness was the key to life. When I went to school, they asked me what I wanted to be when I grew up. I wrote down 'happy.' They told me I didn't understand the assignment, and I told them they didn't understand life." (Anonymous, n.d.).

This is how I want my son, students, pet owner clients, and dogs to live their lives. Live to the fullest, try your best, but never be afraid to make mistakes because there will be many. This is exactly how we (and our dogs) will learn and strive to do better.

It all starts from day one. As a parent and teacher, I knew that encouragement of my son and students from the beginning would lead to their success. This rarely, if ever, proved to be untrue. Jason and my students in school worked hard and to the best of their ability because I pushed them. Was I strict? Absolutely. I always taught - and still do teach - in a firm and fair manner. Anyone I teach knows that I care about them but I will settle for nothing but their best. If you are going to do something, you might as well give it 100 percent in my opinion. What I do understand, though, is that one person's best is different from everyone else's and that is exactly how I function in dog and dog owner training. I also encourage owners to relate to their dogs in the same way.

Building Esteem with Socialization

Starting from day one, extensive socialization sets a puppy up for success for the remainder of his life. As part of this, a puppy should meet as close to 100 different people and as many different dogs of all sizes in the first 12 weeks of his life. This should include all different shapes and sizes of men, women, and children, different races, people with no hair, people wearing sunglasses, hats, backpacks, etc. Here is a list to which I refer my clients so their puppies can cover all the bases, in terms of socialization:

Puppy Socialization Check List

Visual & Noises	Places	Interacting with people	Meeting People		People Sounds
Sirens	Veterinarians	Holding puppy	Men with:	Beards	Talking loudly
Fireworks	Boarding kennels	Touching paws		Hats	Laughing
Car horns	Daycare	Touching muzzle		Sunglasses	Crying
Traffic	Pet shop	Touching ears		Jewelry	Shouting
Thunderstorms	Maneuver & Touch	Touching tail		Helmets	Arguing
Fairs and festivals	Stairs	Hugging puppy		Cigarettes	Children playing
Shopping malls	Escalators	Touching collar	Women with:	Hats	
Busy traffic	Tile	Checking teeth		Sunglasses	Meeting Animals
Crowds of people	Marble	Clipping nails		Jewelry	Puppies
Airplanes	Asphalt	Brushing teeth		Helmets	Male adult dogs
Helicopters	concrete	Checking between pads	Children:	0-2 years	Female adult dogs
Wheelchairs	Grass	Cleaning ears		in strollers	Kittens
Crutches, canes	Sand	Touching rear legs		2-4 years old	Cats
Bicycles	Carpet	Brushing, grooming		4-12 years old	Horses
Skateboards	Wood			13-19 years old	Cow
Radios	Smell		Adults with	Crutches	Sheep
loud cars				Canes	Chickens
Motorbikes				Wheel chairs	Ducks
Parking lots			Elderly Person	Male	
Door bells				Female	
Knocking on doors					
Trucks					
Trains					

Proud Pet Professional Guild Member
The Association for Force Free Pet Professionals
www.PetProfessionalGuild.com

The Pet Professional Guild has given permission for active Guild Members to use this educational piece in their businesses © 2012
Developed & Designed by Leah Roberts, Carol Byrnes & Niki Tudge

© Pet Professional Guild 2012. Reprinted with permission.

(Photo: Tereza Huclova/Shutterstock.com)

Socialization with other dogs and humans is critical for puppies.

Most people have different learning styles and, when taught in a certain way, will have a better chance at success. I know I am a visual learner, while many others are auditory learners. If my husband tries to give me directions about how to do something I have never done before, I stop him immediately as I MUST write it down. If I don't, I will not remember anything he says, much less succeed. In this way I set myself up for success and we must do exactly the same with our dogs. As I have mentioned previously, it is amazing to see how many dog owners think a puppy or new rescue comes to them speaking their language and knowing everything that is expected in his new home. If I got sucked up into a spaceship, taken away, dropped onto another planet where I did not know anyone or speak the language, this would be a perfect depiction of what a dog experiences when he enters a new home. Many puppies are acquired between the ages of 8-12 weeks from breeders and, after a long, harrowing plane ride, spend their first night in an unfamiliar, scary place where they know no one, understand nothing, and may be feeling the anxiety of being separated from their mother and litter mates. Many rescue dogs have been around the block a few times and may have lived with various owners or been on the street for some time. They may have received no training, love, or guidance for their life's entirety. How can we possibly expect them to know what we want from them? Obviously, we cannot.

Dogs come into this world knowing none of the things that many owners presume they should, such as how to go to the bathroom outside, how to sit when cued, how not to chew things, etc. When babies are born, parents accept that along the road they must teach this baby everything such as how to use the potty, how to say 'mama' and 'dada,' how to eat by themselves and a whole plethora of other life skills. When hired at a new job, there is, in most cases, a couple weeks of orientation and training and learning how the job works before someone is placed on his or her own. Dog owners must realize that an 8-week-old puppy is exactly the same. Yes, he knows how to walk and eat (somewhat), but he does not know how to sit on cue and, furthermore, does not even know what the word "sit" means. He does not know how to be patient on leash and not criss-cross in front of us on walks, eat everything in sight, or bite the leash. He does not know what "come" means, especially when there is enticing rabbit poop capturing his attention. Most parents would never get angry at a young baby or child for pooping in their diaper, for spitting up on mom, or for falling over when learning to walk. As effective parents or bosses, we encourage, we teach, and we embolden. Yet on a daily basis I see dog owners getting angry at their dogs for not knowing how to do something that was never taught to them. How is this fair? It is not, of course. As dog owners, we most certainly should have high expectations and standards for our dogs, but not without teaching them what we expect them to do. This is how self-esteem and confidence in humans AND dogs grows exponentially.

It is also critical to realize that when dogs suffer from issues such as fear, anxiety, aggression, or any other difficult behavior problem that owners want changed, there is by no means an overnight fix. There will be many mistakes along the way. I want you to think about your own personality flaws. I know I have plenty! Do you have a short temper? Are you hyper-sensitive? Do you have a hard time expressing your emotions? Think about any issues you have in your personality and I would like you to fix them by tomorrow please. Thank you. What do you mean you cannot do that? Why not? Getting my point? It is not feasible for dogs to "fix" behavior overnight, just like we cannot. It takes time, hard work, support, and patience. With some people, it can take years of therapy and a lot of hard work and self-development to improve upon personality issues. Please keep this in your heart and mind when your dog is struggling with behavior issues that you want fixed in three one-hour sessions.

Teach Me So I Understand

We must take our job as leaders and teachers seriously if we want our children, students, employees and dogs to succeed and to work to their highest potential. As adult leaders, be it as a boss, teacher, or parent, we have a responsibility to teach in a way that our learners will understand and in a manner that they can grow and flourish. As a parent and teacher, I find myself occasionally saying or explaining things to my son, Jason and to my students that I assume they know when in fact I have never previously explained it to them. If I tell Jason to clean his room, his idea of clean and my idea of clean are vastly different so I am not generally happy with the result. If I go to his room with him and specifically explain my idea of clean, it usually works better and is improving every day. His idea of clean is clothes shoved in the drawers and sticking out so the drawer will not even close and maybe some, but not all, toys on the floor. My thought pattern is a little different. I find that the more I thoroughly explain what I want to him, my husband, my students, and the dog owners I work with, learning becomes much easier. When they know what is expected they will be that much closer to achieving higher standards and ultimately, success.

With our dogs, to help them reach their highest potential and give them the self-confidence they so desire and deserve, as owners and trainers, we must lay out exactly what we want in a way that they can understand without scaring or hurting them in the process. Just as I would guide a baby to take his first steps, I would teach and guide a dog to learn a new skill. What are the steps in my teaching a dog a new skill?

> Lure him into it. In other words, show him how it is done by guiding him through it. For example, holding a treat by a dog's nose and guiding back him into a sit position. Reinforcing the behavior. In order for dogs to repeat behaviors, they must be reinforced. This can be done using food, toys, walks, or anything the dog loves.
> Next, use a hand signal with a lure. Reinforce.
> Add the verbal cue, followed by hand signal. Reinforce.
> Begin fading the lure so the dog does not become dependent on seeing the lure to perform the behavior. Reinforce.
> Fade (remove) the hand signal and only use verbal if the dog performs the behavior immediately after the verbal cue is given.

(Photo: WilleeCole Photography/Shutterstock.com)

Luring a dog into the sit position. This is a crucial part to get the training process rolling. The trainer is communicating to the dog what she wants him to do by gently luring him back with a food reward. The second the dog's rear hits the floor, the reward is given.

What are the steps when I teach a human (adult or child) a new skill?

> Explain what is going to be taught.
> Show how it is done, also known as modeling.
> Have the person perform the behavior.
> Reinforce and give feedback.
> Review.

The steps are extremely similar for both humans and dogs (except the explaining step, for obvious reasons). My luring step for dogs could be compared to the modeling step for humans. The one step that is extremely important and repetitive, no matter which species I am working with, is reinforcement. If I do not provide feedback or reinforce the behavior that I desire, the person or dog will have no idea if they are getting it right, if they should continue to do the behavior, or try something else instead.

Explain and Reinforce

Constructive criticism is an extremely useful tool in school, the workplace, and dog training. If I have a boss who screams at me or gives bad evaluations each time I do something that he does not necessarily feel is right, I will be upset, angry, and unfortunately, still in the fog about what he DOES want. On the other hand, if he pulls me aside and informs me in a kind way what I am doing wrong and how to make it right, that will give me the critical information I need to improve. Further, because of the manner in which it was done, I will feel encouraged to work even harder. Being criticized for doing something incorrectly without the corresponding information of how to make it right will not enhance my work. What it will do, though, is serve to increase frustration and lower self-esteem. This is exactly what countless owners are unknowingly doing to their dogs, which is the antecedent to more frustration and continued failure.

Dogs need us to lie out exactly what is expected of them. Since we cannot speak to them in a language that they can understand, we must show them instead and then reinforce or reward the behavior we like so they will continue to do it. Let's take a common behavior like sit, for example. When training a dog to sit, I lure the dog with a treat to get him doing the behavior first. While I am holding the treat by his nose to lure him, he might jump to try to get the treat from my hands. I don't yell "NO!" and smack him on the nose if this happens because that is simply not a language he will understand. What it will do, though, is cause a lot of fear and make him afraid to try anything at all next time. Look at it this way. The dog wants the reward more than anything, so let's show him two different paths he can take and let him decide which one ends with the pot of gold. The first path involves him jumping up in an effort to get the treat. If he does this, I quietly pull the treat back and he gets nothing. By doing this, I have communicated with my actions, "Sorry, jumping won't work to get you what you want." If he sits, however, he hears "Yes!" or a click or whistle followed swiftly by the treat that he was previously attempting to acquire by jumping. I make it VERY clear that if you do the behavior correctly, you will hear praise and get what you want and that if you do not do the behavior correctly, you will get nothing. It is that simple. This, my friends, is how you communicate with dogs. Yelling at them does not work. I am sure it makes YOU feel a heck of a lot better but it is not going to make your dog sit any quicker in the future. In the same vein, the "respect" that many advocates of aversive training so long for will be acquired much more quickly through a courteous collaboration as opposed to a totalitarian dictatorship governed by fear.

How Should I Train?

This leads to a discussion regarding the different methods of training a dog. I will not judge what is right or wrong here, but will instead speak in terms of science and experience. In the 1940s, it was not unheard of to hang a dog to the point of asphyxiation, known as the helicopter technique, as a means of discipline. However, simply because it was done that way for a long time does not earn it the title of the most effective way to train. Just 20 years prior to that, women first received the right to vote and it is safe to say that we have come a long way since then. Would we have had a black President back then? No. Would we have had a chance of having a woman President as we do now in 2016? No. That is what is so wonderful about development. We revamp ideas that perhaps were not the most advantageous for everyone involved at the time. Does hitting or yelling at your dog work to stop behavior? In some cases, yes, just as getting yelled at by a boss would make me stop the behavior I was being punished for. The effectiveness of it, though, comes into question because the boss still may not obtain the behavior he wants. This is because he has not made it clear what is expected and has only punished what is not wanted. As the employee, I will wander around the office fearful and irate, wondering when will be the next time I get corrected and for what, since I still am unclear as to what is expected. This will cause a drop in my self-esteem, morale, effectiveness, and therefore, good results.

The same goes for children. Years ago, it was commonplace to spank your child for doing something wrong and many parents, still today, use this type of punishment to discipline their children. But according to research, spanking and hitting as a means to discipline children can actually slow down cognitive development, lessen their chances of doing well in school, and increase anti-social and criminal behavior. Murray Straus, founder and co-director of the Family Research Lab and professor emeritus of sociology at the University of New Hampshire, has published numerous books and has conducted research for 40 years in defense of why corporal punishment does more harm than good for our children.

"Research shows that spanking corrects misbehavior. But it also shows that spanking does not work better than other modes of correction, such as time out, explaining, and depriving a child of privileges. Moreover, the research clearly shows that the gains from spanking come at a big cost. These include weakening the tie between children and parents and increasing the probability that the child will hit other children and their parents, and as adults, hit a dating or marital partner. Spanking also slows down mental development and lowers the probability of a child doing well in school. More than 100 studies have detailed these side effects of spanking, with more than 90 percent agreement among them. There is probably no other aspect of parenting and child behavior where the results are so consistent." (Straus, Douglas, & Medeiros, 2013)

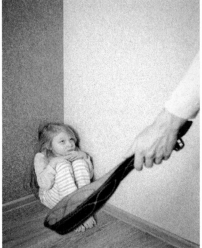

(Photo: Irina Zholudeva/Shutterstock.com)

Spanking has been shown to slow down cognitive development as well as cause fear and other issues. You can see from the child's body language and facial expression how fearful she is.

Surprise, surprise, the same goes for dogs. Research depicts the exact same thing in the dog world. Veterinary researchers have found through a year-long survey of dog owners that those owners who use aversive, confrontational, and harsh methods to train their dogs tend to have dogs that act out aggressively. The study, published in *Applied Animal Behavior Science*, also showed that using non-aversive or neutral training methods such as additional exercise or rewards elicited very few aggressive responses.

"Nationwide, the [number one] reason why dog owners take their pet to a veterinary behaviorist is to manage aggressive behavior," writes Meghan E. Herron, lead author of the study. "Our study demonstrated that many confrontational training methods, whether staring down dogs, striking them or intimidating them with physical manipulation does little to correct improper behavior and can elicit aggressive responses." (Herron, Shofer, & Reisner, 2009).

This is not shocking as it crosses species lines and clearly shows that aggressive methods, in many cases, will elicit aggressive behavior.

Of the 140 surveys completed, the most frequently listed recommendation sources were "self" and "trainers." Several confrontational methods such as "hit or kick dog for undesirable behavior" (43 percent), "growl at dog" (41 percent), "physically force the release of an item from a dog's mouth" (39 percent), "alpha roll" i.e. physically rolling the dog onto his back and holding him (31 percent), "stare at or stare down" (30 percent), "dominance down" i.e. physically forcing the dog down onto his side (29 percent) and "grab dog by jowls and shake" (26 percent) elicited an aggressive response from at least 25 percent of the dogs on which they were attempted. In addition, dogs brought to the hospital for aggressive behavior towards familiar people were more likely to respond aggressively to some confrontational techniques than dogs brought in for other behavioral reasons.

"This study highlights the risk of dominance-based training, which has been made popular by TV, books and punishment-based training advocates," Herron says. "These techniques are fear-eliciting and may lead to owner-directed aggression." (Herron et al., 2009).

Dogs, just like humans, survive and thrive on love, proper guidance, clear expectations and consequences. Not providing these and incorporating punishment is not fair or reasonable to a child, adult, or animal.

In January 2015, I had to get an exercise stress test done in a hospital and this involved sitting on a bike with EKG modules hooked up to me while I kept a mouthpiece connected to a tube in my mouth so the test could record the levels of oxygen and so on. When I started the test, the pulmonary technician told me to breathe normally. Now, with all of this stuff hooked up to me, I was doing the best I could to breathe "normally" but, apparently, I was not. He kept repeating "breathe normal, breathe normal!" in an increasingly aggravated tone. Well, for the life of me, I did not know what I was doing wrong and the frustration on my part was building. He finally said, "Take off the mouth tube! If you don't breathe normally, we can't do the test!" I looked right at him and calmly said, "Then tell me what I am doing wrong and what to do differently, please." He then followed up with, "You are breathing too deep. I need you to breathe shorter breaths." Well, for goodness sake, why didn't you say that in the first place, I was thinking to myself! That would have been so much easier and we would not have had to re-start the test.

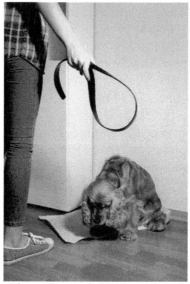

(Photo: Africa Studio/Shutterstock.com)

Harming a dog in the name of training has been shown to lead to fear and aggression issues. This dog is displaying many signs of fear, including cowering into a ball, ears down, head down, and avoiding eye contact with the owner.

This is what our dogs are so desperately longing for. I am going to now take you through some common behavior problems and how to address them without the use of force. Instead you will simply be "speaking dog" and making it 100 percent crystal clear what you want from your dog, just as you would to your child, spouse, or co-worker. Communicating in a manner that dogs can comprehend without the fear of being hurt or frightened in the process will go a long way toward building up their self-esteem.

Stop Barking at Me!

When your dog barks or whines at you for attention, do you answer him? Do you say, "What do you want?" or "Quiet" or "No!"? Really think about it for a minute. Do you think your dog has any idea what you are saying? All he hears is "gh^$*F#(@#!" being yelled in his face. What information is that giving him? Again, it may make our frustration decrease a little but does nothing to make the problem better in the long run. Yelling is a Band Aid and will stop the behavior short-term, but is still not providing the dog with the vital information of what is expected and what will or will not work to get what he wants. He wants attention, plain and simple, and by answering him, you have taught him that he must bark at you to get attention. It does not matter what you say or the tone in which it is said. You are still heavily reinforcing the behavior that you want to cease.

Since your dog wants your attention and is using barking to achieve his goal, show him that the barking will remove your attention EVERY TIME. If every bark in your face makes you walk away, his behavior then becomes counterproductive. Remember though, while you remove your attention every time the demand barking occurs, you are showing the dog what does not work, but he also needs to know what will work. Reinforcing and praising the quiet will make THAT behavior increase in frequency. Again, you are teaching your dog two paths he can take. One path is that exhibiting an undesirable behavior will end up with what he wants being removed and getting no reinforcement whatsoever. The alternative is that the behavior you desire predicts praise, petting, a game, a treat, or any other reinforcement your dog loves! Show him and be perfectly clear about which path will work in his best interest. This also applies to standing at windows or on decks and barking, and other similar contexts. Yelling will not work long-term, but quietly and gently removing the dog from the window or deck and putting him in a crate every time he does it will teach him in a short time that his barking is counterintuitive. You can also call your dog to you and reward him with a game of tug which makes coming away from the distraction and barking much more tempting.

OUCH!!

Play-biting and nipping is another common behavior that can cause a great deal of irritation in dog owners. Puppies are not the only guilty parties when it comes to this behavior and a 70 pound dog putting his teeth on your skin can cause a lot of pain, even in play. If a dog has a habit of nipping during play, do not play with your hands! Use a toy instead. If dogs get reinforced for putting teeth on skin, either through play or being yelled at for the behavior, the nipping can become more frequent and more painful.

Let's look at the two paths that you give your dog to choose from. Some dogs use play biting as a way to garner attention and continue play so the first path will lead to play ending immediately whenever teeth meet skin or clothes. No questions asked. You walk away and it is game over. EVERY TIME. As such, the biting behavior has had the opposite effect and the reinforcement was removed immediately. In addition, this teaches puppies the invaluable lesson of acquired bite inhibition whereby they learn how much pressure they can put down without causing damage.

The alternative path is one where the dog does not chomp down in play and thus the game continues. Make sure you let him know what he is doing right and praise him for playing without the use of his teeth. This is the vital information he needs to continue the desired behavior. If the nipping continues even when ignoring, it you can implement time outs, which can be very effective when used consistently. When teeth playfully bite too hard on skin or clothes, calmly say "time-out" and gently put the dog in a room or crate for two minutes and leave the room. Contrary to popular belief, doing this will not form a negative association to the crate. The take-away for the dog is simply that he is separated from you and your attention for two minutes. If he tries to take off once he gets wise to the time-out scenario, you do not want to get into a struggle of dragging him to the crate or room, so you can simply leave the room for the two minutes instead. The removal of attention is what will make the behavior decrease in frequency and intensity. If the behavior is very strong and has received a lot of reinforcement for some time, it may take a little longer to extinguish. Most dogs take approximately 12 to 20 times before they connect their behavior to the consequence, so do not give up too soon. Remember, in the language of behavioral science, if a behavior stops receiving reinforcement, it will become extinct, so hang in there, be consistent, and make sure everyone in the house is on board. Dogs, like humans, need consistency for success and can easily become confused if rules and structure are constantly changing.

Get Off Me!!

You are all dressed up in your fancy work clothes, walk out of your bedroom, and your dog who was just playing in the muddy backyard comes over and jumps on you leaving a beautiful display of filthy artwork on your white Dolce & Gabbana pants. I don't know about you but that would put me through the roof! Why do dogs jump? Frankly, they are social animals and they get attention for doing so. Many owners will yell at their dogs for jumping, say "off," push them down, or something similar. In the dog's eyes, this is all attention and reinforcement of the behavior. My motto is "no look, no talk, no touch" when dogs are jumping. Implementing any of those three will reinforce the behavior that you are attempting to terminate. If the dog at any time receives visual, verbal (even yelling) or physical contact when jumping on someone, this will reinforce the behavior and make it escalate. Let's travel down the two paths once more. Path one - jump on me for attention and the attention is withdrawn by my turning around or walking away. EVERY TIME. Path two – sit for attention and receive all the attention which you are craving.

Steal and Destruct

For a young, bored, mentally unstimulated dog, slippers or shoes (fill in the blank with television remotes, eye glasses, magazines, etc.) lying out in the open are nothing but an invitation. They might as well have a sign on them that says, "Grab me, run, hide, and rip to shreds past the point of identification." Your 2-year-old child would see the same sign, yes? Remember, your dog is on par with the intelligence of your 2 year-old, so he is seeing the slippers in the exact same way. When it comes to a child, we would most likely put the slippers away so he or she would not have the opportunity to take them. We would manage the situation and set up the child to succeed. Do the same thing with your dog. For a child, you would provide him with many toys to keep him occupied and focused on a task so he would not be bored enough to want the slippers. Do the same with your dog. If your dog has a yummy elk antler, stuffed frozen Kong, marrow bone, Himalayan Yak chew, or another engaging toy to keep his brain focused, the last thing on his mind will be your slippers. We would never expect our children to sit in a room with no toys to keep them engrossed and not reach for, try to play with and/or destroy everything within reach. We must have the same expectations and allowances for our dogs.

Please Don't Hurt Me

Many owners get to the point of no return where they feel they have tried everything and nothing is working, although, as should be apparent by now, communicating in a way your dog understands will produce positive results. I see owners on a daily basis that inform me they have tried to stop behaviors by shaking a can with coins in it, rolling a dog on his back, throwing bean bags at the dog when he does something "wrong," yelling, shocking the dog with a remote, electronic collar, hitting him with a newspaper, holding his mouth shut or sticking their finger in the side of his mouth after nipping, spraying water in the dog's face, and the list goes on and on. Yes, this will stop the behavior for THAT TIME, but it is just a Band Aid that risks the very real, negative side-effects of fear and anxiety. Remember, we need our boss to tell us, not scream at us, what we are doing wrong and, more importantly, inform us what we need to do to make it right. Using aversive methods such as these on our dogs does nothing to give them the information they need to offer the right behavior.

I also hear frequently, "All I have to do is pick up the spray bottle and he knows he did wrong. He looks guilty." What may appear on the surface as guilt is actually fear of the spray bottle. There is no scientific evidence at this point in time that supports the idea of dogs experiencing guilt after doing something we consider wrong. That "guilty" look you are witnessing is fear, either attributed to your body language, tone of voice, or prior punishment in a similar situation. All the punishments listed in the previous paragraph do nothing to provide the dog with the information he needs and only serve to increase fear and anxiety, lower self-esteem, and possibly increase aggressive tendencies.

"The use of such punishing and confrontational methods seems to have grown from the presumption that canine misbehavior or aggression is rooted in the dog's attempt to express social dominance over its owner, and this has been triggered by a lack of assertiveness or authority on the part of that owner," says Stanley Coren, professor of canine psychology at the University of British Columbia in Vancouver, Canada. "Advocates of such theories suggest that dog owners need to establish themselves as the "alpha" or "pack leader," using physical manipulations, threat, and intimidation in order to do so. The application of force is supposed to compel the dog into adopting a less challenging, more compliant, subordinate attitude. These ideas persist even though research has suggested that such beliefs based upon data collected on the behavior of wolves in packs is likely wrong." (Coren, 2012).

There is overwhelming evidence that dogs are at the same intelligence level of a 2-3-year-old human child, which I think many owners may agree with based on their dogs' behavior. This suggests that we could learn a great deal about dogs by studying children in greater depth. As shown earlier, with the negative effects that spanking and hitting children can have, the same conclusions can be drawn for dogs. Physical punishment has the same effect on dogs as it does children, namely that it increases aggressive behavior overall, especially toward the person inflicting the punishment. "Given these findings, recommendations advocating the use of punishing and confrontational methods as part of dog training and behavior control seem to be ill advised." (Coren, 2012).

In 1744, Founding Father Benjamin Franklin, in his *Poor Richard's Almanack,* made these words infamous and they can be applied to everything we do in our everyday interactions with humans AND our dogs: "Tart Words make no Friends: a spoonful of honey will catch more flies than a Gallon of Vinegar." (Franklin, 1744). Think of that the next time you think of hitting your dog for doing something you consider to be wrong instead of rewarding the right behavior.

Empower Me!

If I am teaching a new concept to a student, my son, Jason, or a training client and their dog, I do my best to transfer the power to them because that is how true learning will flourish. If someone is forced to do something, they may perform but in many cases it will be under duress, which is not the most beneficial learning experience. As a parent, I feel it is my responsibility not only to teach Jason but to give him the tools to work things out for himself and become independent and empowered in his own learning. Also, in my past as an employee, the more of the job that was delegated to me and the more trust was placed in me that I could accomplish it without being forced, the more confidence, determination, and fearlessness I had to enable me to move forward and succeed.

I do this on a daily basis with the dog and dog owner students I work with. If I do all the work at every session, the learning will not be internalized and the owner will feel lost once I leave. I follow the steps mentioned previously for teaching a new skill. I explain and model and get to the "doing" step as quickly as possible so the owner can take full ownership of the learning process. I then offer feedback as the owner practices. Do this with your dog too since feedback, as I have already mentioned, is one of the most important yet most overlooked parts of a dog-owner relationship.

When working with a dog, it is critical to provide empowerment, or control, of the learning. This is especially key when working with a dog that is fearful. I work with many dogs that are anxious about being touched or handled in certain ways so this is the perfect time to teach empowerment. If a dog feels in control of his learning, like humans, he will progress at a faster rate than when being coerced. If a dog does not like his paws handled, I will not reach out, grab the paw and start rubbing it as this will accomplish nothing but put the dog over threshold and quite conceivably get myself bitten. You must be smart and patient in a situation like this. I start shaping the dog to give me his paw instead of simply taking the paw. According to Karen Pryor, an American author, specialist in behavioral psychology, and one of the pioneers of clicker training, the word "shaping" is "scientific slang for building a particular behavior by using a series of small steps to achieve it. "Shaping allows you to create behavior from scratch without physical control or corrections, but rather by drawing on your animal's natural ability to learn," says Pryor (2007).

For example, I would hold a treat in my right hand and wait for the dog to paw at it. If he nibbles, bites, licks, or engages in another behavior I do not want, I will ignore it and he will receive no reinforcement. If he paws at my hand, I click/whistle/say 'yes' and reward the behavior. Remember the paths we discussed before? Here they are again. The path of performing the desired behavior will lead to praise and reward. The undesirable behavior path will lead to no praise or reward. Repeat this a few times and your dog will begin to see that touching your hand with his paw is not only fun but that he will never be forced to do it. When he chooses to do it, he will be rewarded and if he chooses not to do it, nothing happens. As the dog becomes more comfortable with handing over his paw, I will move ahead. Moving ahead will only occur, though, when - and only when - the dog shows no signs of discomfort, anxiety, or fear. I want the dog feeling elated about handing over his paw and that is when I know it is time to move on. My next step may be to remove the treat from my hand and allow the dog to place his paw in my open, flat palm for one second. After that is accomplished and I am noting excitement from the dog, I may have him place his paw in my hand for two-three seconds and see the response. Throughout this process, I am listening to everything the dog is telling me with his body language. If he wants to stop, then we stop. If I move too quickly through the process, most dogs will want to stop, which is why I like to move at a pace where the dog feels in control and is without a hint of fear or anxiety. The next step may be having the paw in my hand and rubbing it slightly for one second or less. If at any time the dog pulls the paw away, he is telling me I am moving too fast and I will most absolutely listen. If I don't, I set back the training and halt any forward momentum. The more control the dog feels he has, the better and faster the progress will be.

Our human ego can provide quite the challenge for us to hand over power to an animal but, think about it. We are actually using our power to make the animal think they have the power (which they do) and it works beautifully. It is a win-win. Many times, I hear owners say statements such as, "I'm in charge and he should do what I want." Shoulda, woulda, coulda does not work and it certainly has no place in training our dogs. Hand over empowerment to your dog, show him he has what it takes to improve, as shown in the example of the body handling exercise above, and see what happens. It is a beautiful moment to see an animal feel empowered and unafraid to take part in the learning process. Ultimately, handing over the power in situations like this gives us more power in the long run.

Chapter 7

Putting the Self-Actualization Similarities to Use in Training

"What a man can be, he must be," said Maslow (1954). In the same way, I wholeheartedly believe that what a dog can be, he must be and that we need to guide him on this journey, just as we would our children.

The top level and peak of Maslow's Hierarchy of Needs is self-actualization. Can our dogs self-actualize? Given the fact that many humans do not strive for self-fulfillment and personal growth, it might be a stretch to think of our dogs involved in this type of higher-level thinking. According to Maslow (1943), self-actualization for humans comprises realizing personal potential, self-fulfillment, seeking personal growth and enjoying peak experiences. Do dogs do some of these things? In their own way, absolutely, yes.

For us, self-actualization would include reaching our highest potential and doing the best of which we are capable. Maslow lists the following as characteristics of self-actualization. As you did previously in the *Self-Actualization* section in Chapter 1, ask yourself if you and/or your dog fit any of the descriptions:

> Self-actualized people embrace the unknown and the ambiguous.
> They accept themselves, together with all their flaws.
> They prioritize and enjoy the journey, not just the destination.
> While they are inherently unconventional, they do not seek to shock or disturb.
> They are motivated by growth, not by the satisfaction of needs. They have purpose.
> They are not troubled by the small things. They are grateful.

> They share deep relationships with a few, but also feel identification and affection towards the entire human race. They are humble. They resist enculturation. They are not perfect.

When I read this list, I honestly believe that many dogs exhibit more of these characteristics than some of the many people I have met. Let's take each one and see how it relates to us AND our dogs.

Self-actualized people embrace the unknown and the ambiguous. We all know those people who will try absolutely anything with no fear. They enjoy change and keeping things spontaneous and fun. Some of us have dogs like this as well. My dog Sierra was found on the street and that girl is not afraid of ANYTHING. She is always willing to check something out first and give it a whirl, be it a new toy, meeting a new person, or going to a new place. She embraces every new opportunity. I know plenty of people who will embrace these challenges as she and many other dogs will. We can continue to learn from them.

Self-actualized people accept themselves, together with all their flaws. Watch a confident person walk into a room. You cannot quite put your finger on it, but the level of confidence the person exudes is usually obvious. Dogs can get away with this too. You can clearly see some dogs who are quite comfortable with who they are while others show signs of being not quite settled in a variety of contexts.

Self-actualized people prioritize and enjoy the journey, not just the destination. I know this is something I work on every day. It is quite the challenge as in this day and age life is often more about arriving than striving, and even more so in the New Jersey/New York area where I am based. Things move far quicker here and I often look to Sierra and Jason for reminders to focus on the journey and to stop and smell the roses. This is an area where, as humans, we can most certainly look to our dogs for some guidance. If any being knows how to live in the now, it is our dogs. Stopping to sniff every tree and not having a care in the world while doing so is truly living in the moment and enjoying the journey, for sure.

While they are inherently unconventional, self-actualized people do not seek to shock or disturb. We all know the person who makes waves just to make waves. These people are not fighting for a specific reason or goal, but seem to simply get off on being a rebel. I know dogs do not have the capacity, as far as we know, to think at this level, so this will be left to science and research to explore further.

Self-actualized people are motivated by growth, not by the satisfaction of needs. I tend to believe that dogs are a bit behind humans on this one. They are all about doing what works to get what they want. As much as people think dogs want to please their owners, science shows in most cases, they want to do whatever it will take to get their needs satisfied.

Self-actualized people have purpose. A person with purpose is unstoppable. Nothing can stand in their way and they will not let a road block stop or impede their journey. Give a dog an interactive feeding toy and tell me he does not have purpose. Prove to me that the 9-11 rescue dogs in NYC did not have purpose. A bomb-sniffing dog works with absolute purpose to complete his tasks. Does this mean the dog is living with purpose or just doing what he has been trained to do and working toward the reward at the end? More research is necessary to provide answers to this.

Self-actualized people are not troubled by the small things. What Maslow (1954) terms the "lack of worry over immediate concerns" is very prevalent in the dog world. If I am getting ready for a dressy function, I know I am worried about one hair being out of place, if my dress makes my butt look big, and what purse will match with my outfit. Most dogs, on the other hand, have no issue walking around with slobber swinging from their jowls, prominent eye boogers, and innocently clearing rooms with their gas. If that is not being troubled by the small things, then I want to reach that level of self-actualization because it must be pretty liberating!

<u>Self-actualized people are grateful.</u> Many humans take the pleasures and conveniences in their lives for granted and some are never satisfied no matter what is acquired. It is simply never enough. In contrast, there are other people with virtually nothing who are striving for self-actualization and are more grateful and appreciative for the little they have. There is not sufficient research as of yet to show if dogs feel gratitude, but I would put my money on it that they do. The looks and cuddles I receive from Sierra scream, "thank you for saving me from the street!" Abused and neglected animals who were rescued from the street or used for fighting and then wind up in loving homes have hit the proverbial jackpot. I know many owners who would bet their lives on the fact that their dogs feel gratitude for being rescued, but let's hold out for some studies on this in the future.

(Photo- MyImages: Micha/Shutterstock.com)

A very happy dog who could possibly be showing signs of gratitude (but more research must be done to prove this). This dog is grinning from ear to ear with a "doggy" smile, relaxed ears, soft eyes without dilated pupils, relaxed corners of the mouth, and absence of furrowed brow. THIS is what we want to see in canine body language.

Self-actualized people share deep relationships with a few, but also feel identification and affection towards the entire human race. As I have gotten older, my circle has shrunk quite a bit, mostly by choice. I feel a deep connection to my best friend Bob, also lovingly known as "Boober," and a few others, and would choose to spend more time with them and my family. That in no way means that I do not care about others. I happen to love hearing people talk and learning about their different life experiences, thoughts, and feelings. It fascinates me but, at the end of the day, I prefer the company of a small circle of friends and family. Many dogs are the same. Sierra is the type of dog that will go up to absolutely anyone to say 'hi' and receive petting and cuddles. She is afraid of no one and loves the attention. Even with her outgoing ways, she prefers her family and will always come back to us in a room full of people. The bond and connection is there and is her top priority in situations like this. It is not that I am "alpha," as we have already ascertained. Sierra doesn't run to me because I am her "pack leader." She runs to me because there is a strong bond and loads of trust that has been developed through our collaborative and loving relationship.

Self-actualized people are humble. Observing an egotistical person or someone who has an absolute blast talking about him- or herself makes it very clear that there is an underlying self-esteem issue. Confident and secure people do not need to inform everyone how fabulous they are because it is already apparent in their work and their actions. Some of the most brilliant people in history were some of the most unpretentious souls around. Most dogs live this way, yes, because they do not have the mental capabilities that humans do.

Self-actualized people resist enculturation. According to Maslow, this means making up one's own mind, coming to decisions on one's own, and not following the herd mentality. I know a few of these types of people. I also strive to be the lion, as opposed to the sheep, as challenging as that may be at times in our culture. Many of our dogs can easily pull this off and it is a beautiful thing to watch a creature who does not have a care in the world about what others think.

Self-actualized people are not perfect. Exactly. Not a single one of us is. This is another area in which dogs have risen above the crowd. What is perfection anyway? Who sets the standards for perfection? Improve along the journey and help your dogs do the same. Enjoy that journey and help your dogs do the same. The more you help them do this, the returns are priceless.

Self-Awareness Tests

Animals, such as great apes, dolphins, orcas, rhesus macaques, Eurasian magpies, and a single Asiatic elephant have all shown signs of self-recognition in various tests conducted. Many other animals have been shown to fail at these self-recognition tests, at least until the "Mirror Test" was utilized (Gallup, 1970). This specific test showed that chimpanzees have quite a bit of self-awareness and self-recognition.

The Mirror Test involved positioning chimpanzees in front of a full-length mirror outside their cages, which they were exposed to for 10 days. Reactions ranged from, at the beginning of the 10-day period, attempting to play with what they thought was another chimpanzee to later actually grooming parts of their body they saw in the mirror. In order to show that the chimpanzees had come to realize what they were seeing in the mirror was actually themselves, Gallup developed the "Mark Test. " While under anesthesia to ensure the chimpanzees would have no knowledge of what was being done, a red dot was placed above one eyebrow and another on the top half of the opposite ear. A dye with no odor or irritants was utilized to ensure there were no clues regarding marks on the body. Once out of anesthesia, none of the chimpanzees touched any of the marks. They were then placed in front of the mirror. Upon sight of their reflections, the primates were able to locate, examine and touch the identifying marks on their bodies. Some even looked at their fingers after touching the marks. This was another step in confirming that animals do have an identifying sense of self (Gallup, 1970).

Some people argue that not all animals are as visually acute as others so this was not accepted as the be-all and end-all of self-recognition tests. Since dogs had not successfully been able to pass the Mirror Test, animal behavior expert Marc Bekoff then implemented the "Yellow Snow" test. Bekoff felt that since dogs' strongest sense is olfactory, that may be where their self-recognition strengths lie. In the Yellow Snow test, Bekoff took urine samples from his own dog, Jethro, as well as other dogs and placed them along the route of a walk he then took with Jethro. Jethro had not seen the placement of the urine samples. During the walk, Bekoff observed closely how long Jethro sniffed each sample and if he urinated on the samples. Jethro seemed generally disinterested in his own urine but did spend an expected amount of time sniffing and marking over the other samples. This led Bekoff to conclude that Jethro displayed a sense of self in being able to decipher his own urine from others. (Bekoff, 2009). With a test group of one, though, most were not convinced.

Evolutionary biologist Roberto Cazzolla Gatti at Tomsk State University, Russia took this research a step further and developed what was called the "Sniff Test of Self-Recognition." Gatti took four urine samples from stray dogs and presented them to the dogs four times a year at the beginning of each new season.

"I placed within a fence five urine samples containing the scent of each of the four dogs and a 'blank sample,' filled only with cotton wool odourless," says Gatti. "The containers were then opened and each dog was individually introduced to the inside of the cage and allowed to freely move for five minutes. The time taken by each dog to sniff each sample was recorded." (Gatti, 2015).

Similar to Bekoff's dog in the Yellow Snow test, each dog spent a longer time smelling other dogs' urine than their own, which again gives credence to the fact that dogs are fully aware of their own scent and have little interest in sniffing and marking their own urine. What was very interesting in Gatti's test was that the older the dog, the stronger the results, showing that self-awareness in dogs may actually increase with age.

There is a lot more research and testing to be conducted before this self-actualization piece can be fully accepted as part of the *Hierarchy of Needs* for dogs, but the tests and observations do lean in the favor of dogs exhibiting human-like characteristics even at this top level of the hierarchy.

Listen and Learn

I do not consider myself a religious person but tend to lead a very spiritual life nonetheless. In 2015 I took part in a soul level (i.e. deep intuitive connection, not superficial) course in animal communication at the Omega Institute in Rhinebeck, New York with the amazing and world-renowned animal intuitor and intuitive coach, Danielle MacKinnon. MacKinnon shared a very important piece of information as part of the basis for the course: That animals are here to teach us. I wholeheartedly believe this. Humans seem to have this notion that they are the superior being but, in fact, animals are the ones who have reached the level of unconditional love that we, as human beings, strive for. The more we listen to our dogs, observe them, and learn from them, the more sophisticated we can - and will - become as a species. I fully believe that animals do not come into our lives by accident and that our dogs (and other pets for that matter) are with us for a reason. Some pet owners might think it is to drive them crazy while others may think it is to help them get through a major life change or struggle, such as illness or loss of a loved one.

What I do know is that with every dog I have ever owned, trained, or come into contact with, I have walked away learning something. Many owners share with me the struggles they have in their own lives and, many times, it seems as if the dog is behaving in a way that will help his owner. This might include working on what might be a less desirable personality trait. Perhaps a highly reactive dog is teaching his owner how to be more patient. Maybe that fearful, shy, and anxious dog you adopted is teaching you how to work on your own insecurities.

I believe that the more we work together with our dogs, the more we can learn from them and them from us. We are here to help and guide them and they are here to do the same for us. By looking at the relationship in this way, we can create a more positive, collaborative bond as opposed to one that is based on fear and the outdated notion of pack leadership. I hope this has helped you to realize how similar your dog really is to you and I wish you the utmost in a successful, happy, relaxed life with your dog!

REFERENCES

Abraham Maslow Quotes. (n.d.). Retrieved December 12, 2015, from
http://www.azquotes.com/author/9574-Abraham_Maslow

Alvin Price Quotes. (n.d.). *Quotes.net*. Retrieved February 19, 2016, from
http://www.quotes.net/quote/16511

American Psychological Association. (2009, August 10). Dogs' Intelligence On
Par With Two-year-old Human, Canine Researcher Says. *ScienceDaily*. Retrieved
January 27, 2016, from
www.sciencedaily.com/releases/2009/08/090810025241.htm

American Veterinary Dental College. (1988). Periodontal Disease. Retrieved
February 10, 2016, from http://www.avdc.org/periodontaldisease.html

Andics, A., Gácsi, M., Faragó, T., Kis, A., & Miklósi, Á. (2014). Voice-Sensitive
Regions in the Dog and Human Brain Are Revealed by Comparative fMRI.
Current Biology, 24(5), 574-578. Retrieved November 22, 2015, from
http://www.cell.com/current-biology/abstract/S0960-9822(14)00123-7

Archer, J. (1997, July). Why do people love their pets? *Evolution and Human
Behavior*, 18 (4), 237-259. Retrieved January 10, 2016, from
http://www.ehbonline.org/article/S0162-3095(99)80001-4/abstract

Bekoff, M., Allen, C., & Burghardt, G. M. (2002). The cognitive animal: Empirical
and theoretical perspectives on animal cognition. Cambridge, MA: MIT Press

Bekoff, M. (2009, June 29). Hidden tales of yellow snow: What a dog's nose
knows - Making sense of scents. *Psychology Today*. Retrieved December 28,
2015, from https://www.psychologytoday.com/blog/animal-
emotions/200906/hidden-tales-yellow-snow-what-dogs-nose-knows-making-
sense-scents

Bekoff, M. (2015). Playful fun in dogs. *Current Biology, 21*(1), R4-R7. Retrieved
February 12, 2016, from http://www.cell.com/current-biology/abstract/S0960-
9822(14)01122-
1?_returnURL=http://linkinghub.elsevier.com/retrieve/pii/S09609822140112
21?showall=true

Berns, G. S., Brooks, A. M., & Spivak, M. (2012). Functional MRI in Awake
Unrestrained Dogs. *PLoS ONE, 7*(5). Retrieved December 30, 2015, from
http://journals.plos.org/plosone/article?id=10.1371/journal.pone.0038027

Berns, G. (2013, October 5). Dogs Are People, Too. Retrieved November 23,
2015, from http://www.nytimes.com/2013/10/06/opinion/sunday/dogs-are-
people-too.html?pagewanted=all&_r=1&

Berns, G. S., Brooks, A. M., & Spivak, M. (2015). Scent of the familiar: An fMRI study of canine brain responses to familiar and unfamiliar human and dog odors. *Behavioural Processes, 110*, 37-46. Retrieved January 9, 2016, from http://www.sciencedirect.com/science/article/pii/S0376635714000473

Chijiwa, H., Kuroshima, H., Hori, Y., Anderson, J. R., & Fajita, K. (2015). Dogs avoid people who behave negatively to their owner: Third-party affective evaluation. *Animal Behavior, 106*, 123-127. Retrieved January 2, 2016, from http://www.sciencedirect.com/science/article/pii/S0003347215001979

Cohen, P. (2012, December 17). Poverty Poses a Bigger Risk to Pregnancy Than Age Does. Retrieved February 26, 2016, from http://www.theatlantic.com/sexes/archive/2012/12/poverty-poses-a-bigger-risk-to-pregnancy-than-age-does/266348/

Coren, S. (2009, August 8). Smarter Than You Think: Renowned Canine Researcher Puts Dogs' Intelligence on Par with 2-Year-Old Human. Retrieved October 2, 2015, from http://www.apa.org/news/press/releases/2009/08/dogs-think.aspx

Coren, S. (2012, May 24). Is Punishment An Effective Way To Change The Behavior Of Dogs? Retrieved January 8, 2016, from https://www.psychologytoday.com/blog/canine-corner/201205/is-punishment-effective-way-change-the-behavior-dogs

Couppis, M. H., & Kennedy, C. H. (2008). The rewarding effect of aggression is reduced by nucleus accumbens dopamine receptor antagonism in mice. *Psychopharmacology, 197*(3), 449-456. Retrieved February 14, 2016, from http://link.springer.com/article/10.1007/s00213-007-1054-y

Davis, E. P., Glynn, L. M., Waffarn, F., & Sandman, C. A. (2011). Prenatal maternal stress programs infant stress regulation. *Journal of Child Psychology and Psychiatry, 52*(2), 119-129. Retrieved February 5, 2016, from http://onlinelibrary.wiley.com/doi/10.1111/j.1469-7610.2010.02314.x/full

Dewey, R. (2007). Conditional Emotional Responses. Retrieved December 12, 2016, from http://www.intropsych.com/ch05_conditioning/conditional_emotional_responses.html

Dockrill, P. (2015, December 17). Dogs give food to their 'friends' in first-of-its-kind study. Retrieved December 10, 2015, from http://www.sciencealert.com/dogs-give-food-to-their-friends-in-first-of-its-kind-study

Eckstein, S. (2009). Depression In Dogs. *WebMD*. Retrieved December 30, 2015, from http://pets.webmd.com/dogs/features/depression-in-dogs?page=2

Enayati, A. (2012, June 1). The Importance of Belonging. *CNN*. Retrieved January 1, 2016, from http://www.cnn.com/2012/06/01/health/enayati-importance-of-belonging/

Fisher, T. (2014, November). Brain Scans Reveal What Dogs Really Think of Us. *Scientists.Mic*. Retrieved December 5, 2015, from http://mic.com/articles/104474/brain-scans-reveal-what-dogs-really-think-of-us#.BYJJZRvit

Fulghum, R. (n.d.). BrainyQuote.com. Retrieved February 26, 2016, from http://www.brainyquote.com/quotes/quotes/r/robertfulg106965.html

Gácsi, M., Gyoöri, B., Virányi, Z., Kubinyi, E., Range, F., Belényi, B., & Miklósi, Á. (2009). Explaining Dog Wolf Differences in Utilizing Human Pointing Gestures: Selection for Synergistic Shifts in the Development of Some Social Skills. *PLoS ONE, 4*(9). Retrieved January 17, 2016, from http://journals.plos.org/plosone/article?id=10.1371/annotation/9d7a0174-3068-4c44-bb98-b8a9bc5a99d5

Gallup, G. G. (1970). Chimpanzees: Self-Recognition. *Science, 167*(3914), 86–87. Retrieved January 7, 2016, from http://www.jstor.org/stable/1728199

Gatti, R. C. (2015, November 13). Self-consciousness: Beyond the looking-glass and what dogs found there. *Taylor & Francies Online*. Retrieved February 16, 2016, from http://www.tandfonline.com/doi/full/10.1080/03949370.2015.1102777

Gatti, R.C. (2015, November 22). Dogs (and probably many other animals) have a conscience too! Retrieved January 9, 2016, from http://robertocazzollagatti.com/2015/11/22/dogs-and-probably-many-other-animals-have-a-conscience-too/

Grimm, D. (2014, May 19). In dogs' play, researchers see honesty and deceit, perhaps something like morality. *Washington Post*. Retrieved July 27, 2015, from https://www.washingtonpost.com/national/health-science/in-dogs-play-researchers-see-honesty-and-deceit-perhaps-something-like-morality/2014/05/19/d8367214-ccb3-11e3-95f7-7ecdde72d2ea_story.html

Groves, C.P. (1999). *The advantages and disadvantages of being domesticated. Perspectives in Human Biology, 4*, 1-12

Hare, B., & Woods, V. (2013). The Genius of Dogs: How Dogs Are Smarter Than You Think. New York, NY: The Penguin Group.

Harris, C. R., & Prouvost, C. (2014). Jealousy in Dogs. *PLoS ONE, 9*(7). Retrieved January 4, 2016, from http://journals.plos.org/plosone/article?id=10.1371/journal.pone.0094597

Hekman, J., DVM, MS. (2014, November). How a Mother's Stress Can Influence Unborn Puppies. *The Whole Dog Journal*. Retrieved December 7, 2015, from http://www.whole-dog-journal.com/issues/17_11/features/How-a-Mothers-Stress-can-Influence-Unborn-Puppies_21078-1.html

Herron, M. E., Shofer, F. S., & Reisner, I. R. (2009). Survey of the use and outcome of confrontational and non-confrontational training methods in client-owned dogs showing undesired behaviors. *Applied Animal Behaviour Science, 117*(1-2), 47-54. Retrieved October 3, 2015, from http://www.appliedanimalbehaviour.com/article/S0168-1591(08)00371-7/abstract

Hetts, S., & Estep, D. Q. (2007). Myth Of Reinforcing Fear. Retrieved December 1, 2015, from http://fearfuldogs.com/myth-of-reinforcing-fear/

Hoffman, E. (1988). The Right to be Human: A Biography of Abraham Maslow. NY: St. Martin's Press.

Joyce, R. (2013, March 15). Which Came First? The Dog or the Master? Retrieved December 1, 2015, from https://www.psychologytoday.com/blog/what-makes-us-human/201303/which-came-first-the-dog-or-the-master

Kogan, L. R., Schoenfeld-Tacher, R., & Simon, A. A. (2012). Behavioral effects of auditory stimulation on kenneled dogs. *Journal of Veterinary Behavior, 7*, 268-275. Retrieved February 2, 2016, from http://www.news.colostate.edu/content/documents/Behavioral effects of auditory stimulation on kenneled dogs published.pdf

Manning, S. (2016, January 13). 'Fear-free' veterinarians aim to reduce stress for pets. *Associated Press: The Big Story*. Retrieved January 31, 2016, from http://bigstory.ap.org/article/3f8130450d6440c797db54cbca51dcdb/fear-free-veterinarians-aim-reduce-stress-pets

Maslow, A. H. (1954). Motivation and Personality. Retrieved February 10, 2016, from http://scottbarrykaufman.com/wp-content/uploads/2015/01/Maslow-1954.pdf

Maslow, A. (1968). Toward A Psychology of Being. US: Start Publishing LLC, New York, NY

Mayo Clinic. (2013, June 19). Nearly 7 in 10 Americans Take Prescription Drugs, Mayo Clinic, Olmsted Medical Center Find. Retrieved September 3, 2015, from http://newsnetwork.mayoclinic.org/discussion/nearly-7-in-10-americans-take-prescription-drugs-mayo-clinic-olmsted-medical-center-find/

McConnell, A. R., Brown, C. M., Shoda, T. M., Stayton, L. E., & Martin, C. E. (2011). Friends With Benefits: On the Positive Consequences of Pet Ownership. *Journal of Personality and Social Psychology, 101*(6), 1239-1252. Retrieved October 5, 2015, from https://www.apa.org/pubs/journals/releases/psp-101-6-1239.pdf.

Mech, L. (2000). Leadership In Wolf, Canis lupus, Packs. Retrieved February 10, 2016, from http://www.wolf.org/wp-content/uploads/2013/08/247Leadership.pdf

Mech, L. (n.d.). Wolf News and Info. Retrieved February 10, 2016, from http://www.davemech.org/news.html

Miller, P. (2011, December). De-bunking the "Alpha Dog" Theory. *The Whole Dog Journal*. Retrieved November 10, 2015, from http://www.whole-dog-journal.com/issues/14_12/features/Alpha-Dogs_20416-1.html

Millstein, S. (2014, July 24). Are Dogs Like Humans? Study Finds Pooches Get Jealous, Just Like Us. Retrieved May 25, 2015, from http://www.bustle.com/articles/33146-are-dogs-like-humans-study-finds-pooches-get-jealous-just-like-us

Overall, K. (2016, January). #PPGSummit 2015: Advocating for Change/Interviewer Susan Nilson [Transcript]. *BARKS from the Guild*, p.12-14. Retrieved March 6, 2016, from https://issuu.com/petprofessionalguild/docs/barks_from_the_guild_january_20 16/12

Palagi, E., Nicotra, V., & Cordoni, G. (2015). Rapid mimicry and emotional contagion in domestic dogs. *Royal Society Open Science*. Retrieved December 23, 2015, from http://rsos.royalsocietypublishing.org/content/2/12/150505

Pappas, S. (2014, February 24). The Truth About How Mom's Stress Affects Baby's Brain. *LiveScience*. Retrieved December 8, 2015, from http://www.livescience.com/43579-poverty-stress-infant-development.html

Parker, M. (2015, October 9). Houzz Pets Survey: Who Rules the House — Dogs or Cats? Retrieved February 15, 2016, from http://www.houzz.com/ideabooks/54861101

Perry, B. D. (2006, Summer). Fear and Learning: Trauma-Related Factors in the Adult Education Process. Retrieved February 26, 2016, from http://kimberlysheppard.wiki.westga.edu/file/view/Fear and learning - Trauma-related factors in the adult educational process.pdf

Pryor, K. (2007, April 10). The Shape of Shaping: Some Historical Notes. Retrieved January 6, 2016, from http://www.clickertraining.com/node/1135

Range, F., Quervel-Chaumette, M., Dale, R., & Marshall-Pescini, S. (2015). Familiarity affects other-regarding preferences in pet dogs. *Scientific Reports 5,*

Article Number 18102. Retrieved February 1, 2016, from
http://www.nature.com/articles/srep18102

Seamless Corporate Accounts. (2014, March). The Power of Food. Retrieved
February 1, 2016, from
http://pages.c.seamless.com/rs/seamless/images/COR_041614_OfficeFoodSurv
ey2014_Final.pdf

Soproni, K., Miklósi, Á, Topál, J., & Csányi, V. (2001). Comprehension of Human
Communicative Signs in Pet Dogs (Canis familiaris). *Journal of Comparative
Psychology, 115*(2), 122-126. Retrieved January 5, 2016, from
http://www.cogs.indiana.edu/spackled/2005readings/Sopronietal2001.pdf

Straus, M. A., Douglas, E. M., & Medeiros, R. A. (2013). The Primordial Violence:
Spanking Children, Psychological Development, Violence, and Crime. New York,
NY: Routledge.

Szalavitz, M. (2013, April 16). How Terror Hijacks the Brain. *TIME.com.*
Retrieved January 4, 2016, from http://healthland.time.com/2013/04/16/how-
terror-hijacks-the-brain/

Sze, D. (2015, July 21). Maslow: The 12 Characteristics of a Self-Actualized
Person. *Huffington Post.* Retrieved January 7, 2016, from
http://www.huffingtonpost.com/david-sze/maslow-the-12-
characteris_b_7836836.html

Taylor, C. A., Manganello, J. A., Lee, S. J., & Rice, J. C. (2010). Mothers' Spanking of
3-Year-Old Children and Subsequent Risk of Children's Aggressive Behavior.
Pediatrics, 125(5). Retrieved January 3, 2016, from
http://pediatrics.aappublications.org/content/early/2010/04/12/peds.2009-
2678.info

Tsavoussis, A., Stawicki, S. P., Stoicea, N., & Papadimos, T. J. (2014). Child-
Witnessed Domestic Violence and its Adverse Effects on Brain Development: A
Call for Societal Self-Examination and Awareness. *Frontiers in Public Health,
2*(178). Retrieved December 6, 2015, from
http://www.ncbi.nlm.nih.gov/pmc/articles/PMC4193214/

Turner, C. (2015, December 23). Dogs can imitate each other's expressions just
like humans, study finds. *The Daily Telegraph.* Retrieved January 8, 2016, from
http://www.telegraph.co.uk/news/science/science-news/12066526/Dogs-can-
imitate-each-others-expressions-just-like-humans-study-finds.html

University of Alabama Parenting Assistance Line. (n.d.). Discipline & Guidance
Consistency: An Essential Ingredient. Retrieved February 2, 2016, from
http://www.pal.ua.edu/discipline/consistency.php

University Of New Hampshire. (2013, December 11). Renowned UNH Researcher on Corporal Punishment Makes Definitive Case Against Spanking in New Book. Retrieved February 16, 2016, from http://www.unh.edu/news/releases/2013/12/lw11spanking.cfm

Vanderbilt University. (2008, January 14). Aggression as rewarding as sex, food and drugs. Retrieved January 6, 2015, from http://www.eurekalert.org/pub_releases/2008-01/vu-aar011408.php

Veterinary Medicine and Biomedical Sciences Texas A&M University. (2012, November 15). Benefits of Exercising With Your Dog. Retrieved September 15, 2015, from https://vetmed.tamu.edu/news/pet-talk/benefits-of-exercising-with-your-dog

Walton, G. M., Cohen, G. L., & Garcia, J. (2007). Identity, Belonging, and Achievement. Retrieved February 16, 2016, from http://www.psychologicalscience.org/JOURNALS/CD/17_6_INPRESS/COHEN.PDF

Web MD. (n.d.). Exercise for Dogs. Retrieved January 25, 2016, from http://pets.webmd.com/dogs/guide/exercise-dogs

Williams, Y. (n.d.). Extinction Burst in Psychology: Definition & Examples. Retrieved December 15, 2015, from http://study.com/academy/lesson/extinction-burst-in-psychology-definition-examples-quiz.html

About the Author

Mary Jean Alsina, CPDT-KA, PCT-A, M.A., is a certified professional science-based dog trainer with over 10 years' experience. During this time, she has worked with hundreds and hundreds of dogs exhibiting issues ranging from typical puppy behavior to severe fear and aggression as adults. Alsina is a former New Jersey public school teacher who taught instrumental music (band and strings) for 20 years. She also has an extensive knowledge of the human and canine learning process. Alsina finds the similarities between humans and dogs fascinating and draws on them daily to help her clients in her belief that utilizing the knowledge people use to function and relate to others can easily translate to our relationships with dogs, leading to a more successful and understanding partnership.

Alsina serves on the Steering Committee for the Pet Professional Guild, an international association for force-free animal behavior and training professionals, writes for the Pet Professional Guild's quarterly publication, BARKS from the Guild, and has written for Examiner.com. She has also spoken publicly in a variety of venues on dog behavior and training. Along with holding two graduate degrees in Education and being a Certified

Professional Dog Trainer (CPDT-KA), Alsina was also one of the first 27 Accredited Professionals to earn the title of PCT-A (Professional Canine Trainer-Accredited) through the Pet Professional Accreditation Board.

Alsina is the Founder, Owner, and Head Trainer for The Canine Cure, LLC, a New Jersey- and New York City-based dog training business. She lives in northern New Jersey with her husband Izzy, son Jason, rescue dog Sierra, and many of Sierra's canine friends that come to stay on vacation when their parents travel.

CPSIA information can be obtained
at www.ICGtesting.com
Printed in the USA
FSOW04n0723110916
24871FS

9 781506 901855